POST-ABORTION SYNDROME

Post-Abortion Syndrome

ITS WIDE RAMIFICATIONS

EDITED BY

Peter Doherty

FOUR COURTS PRESS

This book was typeset by
Gilbert Gough Typesetting, Dublin, in
11 on 12.5 point Ehrhardt for
FOUR COURTS PRESS LTD
Kill Lane, Blackrock, Co. Dublin
and in North America by
FOUR COURTS PRESS LTD
c/o ISBS, 5804 NE Hassalo Street, Portland, 0297213

© Individual contributors and Four Courts Press 1995

A catalogue record for this book
is available from the British Library.

ISBN 1-85182-159-7

All rights reserved. No part of this publication may be
reproduced or transmitted in any form or by any means,
including photocopying and recording, without written
permission of the publisher and the individual contributors.
Such written permission must also be obtained before any
part of this publication is stored in a retrieval system
of any nature.

Printed in Great Britain by
Cambridge University Press, Cambridge

Contents

INTRODUCTION
   Peter Doherty   7

POST-ABORTION SYNDROME: A VARIANT OF
   POST-TRAUMATIC STRESS DISORDER
   Vincent M. Rue   15

POST-ABORTION SYNDROME
   Sandro Gindro   29

SELECTION AND INTERPRETATION BIAS IN
   POST-ABORTION RESEARCH
   Mary A. Greenwold, David B. Larson, John S. Lyons and
      Kimberly A. Sherrill   39

POST-ABORTION SYNDROME . . . IS IT A REALITY?
   METHODOLOGICAL ISSUES
   C.V.R. Blacker   47

ABORTION: PSYCHOLOGICAL INDICATIONS AND
   CONSEQUENCES
   Agneta Sutton   55

ONE DOCTOR'S EXPERIENCE
   Margaret White   65

TREATMENT OF POST-ABORTION SYNDROME
   Patricia Casey   73

RELATIONSHIP BETWEEN INDUCED ABORTION AND
CHILD ABUSE AND NEGLECT: FOUR STUDIES
    Philip G. Ney, Tak Fung and Adele Rose Wickett   83

METHODOLOGICAL CONSIDERATIONS IN EMPIRICAL
RESEARCH ON ABORTION
    Rachel L. Anderson, David C. Hanely, David B. Larson and
        Roger C. Sider   103

LIST OF CONTRIBUTORS   117

Introduction

PETER DOHERTY

The Abortion Act of 1967 was introduced in Britain as the result of a well-planned campaign over the preceding 30 years to extend the grounds on which a pregnancy could be terminated. It increased the freedom of women to choose an abortion, the so-called 'right to choose', but limited the freedom of doctors to advise them in the light of all the clinical, social and ethical considerations surrounding their case.

A prime reason for the introduction of the Act was to reduce the number of deaths from illegal abortions, but the maternal death rate per million maternities had already declined appreciably before 1967 and the number of hospital discharges after abortions other than legal, including miscarriages, rose slightly as a proportion of live births, after the Act had been introduced. Criminal activity had been reduced but not ended. The Act did not legalise abortion, which remains a criminal offence. It created exceptions by providing that an offence is not committed when pregnancy is terminated under certain circumstances. Perhaps its most ambiguous provision is that a pregnancy may be terminated if its continuance would involve risk to the life or health of a pregnant mother greater than if the pregnancy were terminated. The inclusion of this provision effectively frustrated any intention of a merely moderate extension to the grounds for termination; 'the physical or mental health of the mother' became the main diagnosis on which the procedure was to be offered.

Thus any trivial liberal interpretation of the Act was permissible, embracing the women's social circumstances either now or in the future. Abortion on demand was not the intention of the legislature at the time but there can be little doubt that society now regards it as woman's right and the medical profession is expected to comply. David Painton states that when women in England and Wales consult a doctor about an unwanted pregnancy, most feel they have already made the decision; no more than 20 per cent ask the doctor if abortion is appropriate.[1] The Act allows abortion

1. Ciba Symposium, No. 115, *Abortion: Medical Progress and Social Implications* (London, 1985).

if the life of the woman is in danger or if the fetus is likely to be severely handicapped, but no more than 2 per cent of abortions are done for these reasons. The vast majority are performed to protect the woman's mental health and, in considering this, account must be taken of the woman's actual or foreseeable environment, or that of her children. The woman does not have to have a mental illness at the time of the abortion but there must be factors in her personality or circumstances that would threaten her mental health if the pregnancy were to continue. It is not surprising therefore that 98 per cent of abortions are performed for social reasons and the procedure itself can be regarded as a form of social engineering. But social evils are best dealt with by attending to their causes and the elimination of an innocent human life is not a suitable way of dealing with them.

The physical complications of abortion—cervical incompetence, pelvic inflammatory disease, with the future possibility of ectopic pregnancies or sterility—have been well documented. But it is only now, after almost 30 years, that the psychiatric complications are becoming more evident. In any controlled trial the disadvantages of a procedure, as well as unforeseen benefits, often become apparent only after a prolonged period. If the abortion procedure is so considered, the hazards, both to the health and future motherhood of the woman and to her existing children, have been evaluated with increasing authority. When the Act was passed its emphasis was thought to be entirely concerned with the elimination of an 'unwanted pregnancy'. It is now recognised that, while abortion kills children, the ethical, social and eugenic principles on which it is based lead to damage to the health, status and integrity of women.

To appreciate this fully it is necessary to review 'attachment behaviour', a concept referring to what is at the basis of the mother and child relationship. All relationships between humans, and indeed between animals, stem from the tendency to form an affectionate bond with a mothering figure or her substitute. It is observable initially during the first year of life and manifests itself as an ability to recognise the mother and to prefer her presence to that of others including the father. Naturally as the child matures others such as the father, siblings or even toys, play an important part in attachment behaviour, but its harmonious progression is an essential feature of normal development. Survival would be impossible without it. Special features are the expression of strong feelings towards the mother ranging from affection, pleasure and satisfaction to frustration and rage.

But as with all special relationships it includes certain fragilities. The full development of the attachment and its persistence can be disrupted by maternal rejection of the child. The mother may be unable to assume her role either because of illness, possibly of a psychiatric nature, or because of a physical condition which prevents her from fulfilling her role; there may be repeated absences which prevent the attachment from flowering; or marital disharmony or other family disturbances may provoke the well-recognised syndrome of separation anxiety. This has been described by John Bowlby as a mixture of tears, anger and hope that the mother may return after she has been persistently absent, progressing into despair when she fails to appear. The child becomes sad, quiet and withdrawn, ultimately moving into a state of detachment which appears to be the child's manifestation of grief and mourning.

The attachment of the mother to her baby commences when she first realises she is pregnant. It may not at this stage reach the full level of personal consciousness, but develops gradually as the pregnancy proceeds. Her thoughts are dominated by the change in her status, and fears may develop about the safety of her future baby. The optimum outlook in a loving relationship is the birth of a healthy baby, to which mother and father become inseparably attached.

But basic maternal feelings that lie at the root of attachment or bonding vary in degree and very often depend on the mother's relationship with the father of the child. When that relationship is one of hostility and abuse the maternal feelings may be correspondingly suppressed and the baby regarded as a hostile intruder. Pregnancies that have resulted from the unconscious need to solve problems such as loneliness, depression or unaccepted parental or social values may not initially arouse strong maternal feelings but frequently do so as the pregnancy proceeds. In these instances a polarity develops between the progressive bonding of the mother with the baby as the pregnancy develops and the reality of a termination.

Are the social and psychogenic factors sufficiently dominant for a fully informed decision to destroy the baby which has been conceived with at least a minimum degree of voluntariness? Clinical experience demonstrates that the decision is seldom fully informed and is made when the mother is probably heavily disturbed. The fact that 98 per cent of abortions are performed for social reasons lends evidence to this view. And among the social reasons perhaps the most dominant factor is severe pressure from husband, boyfriend or mother to have the operation. In the face of such pressure it is difficult to conceive that a balanced decision could be made, one which it should be remembered is made within a very short space of time, usually a matter of weeks.

Anxiety is an excitability which fogs or fouls our rationality; it imperils freedom by limiting choice. Decisions made under its umbrella are inevitably followed by depression.

Even in circumstances, when a woman spontaneously loses a baby after a period of several months of pregnancy, not only does she experience grief at the time of the loss, but she may also experience depression later at the time the baby would have been born.[2]

Grief and mourning are the normal psychological reactions to loss and its commonest manifestation follows bereavement particularly in situations where the loss has been sudden or unexpected. Only after a prolonged period of mourning does the picture become remotely bearable. The loss of a baby in whatever circumstances and at an early stage of pregnancy cannot be an exception.

> Grief is itself a medicine.
> (William Cowper)

In its acute form the loss of a baby through abortion is accompanied by crying spells, insomnia, anguish and sadness together with a preoccupation with the precipitating event. Over a period of time mourning takes over, depending on the personality of the person and the supportive or environmental resources available. Unless the mourning process is allowed to develop and gain a possible level of acceptance by the person the acute symptoms persist as a serious problem. On the other hand we are told by psychiatrists that grief and mourning do not automatically appear and the experience of loss is frequently suppressed. Just as in the physical order it is instinctive to withdraw from pain, it is psychologically protective to withdraw from stress. A mechanism known as 'psychic numbing' buries the memory of the stressful event in a remote corner of the psyche, together with all its stresses and anxieties, thus enabling the persons to present a reasonably calm exterior. But clinical experience regularly shows that a degree of anxiety and depression may re-emerge later.

Underlying this normal psychological reaction of grief and mourning lurks guilt.

> What charm can soothe her melancholy,
> What art can wash her guilty away?
> (Oliver Goldsmith)

But in many of those who have experienced abortions, neither charm nor art are capable of removing the guilt feelings associated with them. Although they have not transgressed the law, for the procedure was performed in accordance with current law, the feelings may remain and be a potent motivating factor in future behaviour. If the choice was made

2. N. Walsh, 'Psychological Aspects of termination of Pregnancy' in *Ethical Issues in Reproductive Medicine* (Dublin, 1982).

regretfully and as a 'last resort' it would not be surprising that a strong element of guilt is generated. As there is an interrelationship between guilt, hostility and anxiety, the emergent anxiety following a termination may have guilt as its root. For those who consider the procedure as an assault on the inviolable right to life of the fetus, and a serious personal offence against God's ultimate authority, it can be expected that guilt feelings, often severe, will occur, and can be regarded as a proportionate psychological reaction to perceived serious transgression of an objective moral code.

That this may occur is not necessarily confined to those with strong religious beliefs but has been evidenced throughout history. It would be odd if something so fundamental as killing another human being were not recognised, whatever the impediments of false moral beliefs (e.g. 'Abortion is a straigtforward exercise of woman's "right to choose"'), as a grave transgression of a moral order to which we all owe allegiance. The recognition may be obscured but is unlikely to be obliterated in any other than those who have completely given themselves over to wickedness. If so, the experience of guilt in some form is likely to emerge first in virtue of the grave and fundamental character of the moral transgression involved in abortion.

Furthermore what is at issue in abortion is not just 'killing an innocent human being' but 'killing a child who has come into existence precisely through one's capacity to be a mother': the one killed had a unique claim precisely on one's maternal attachment.

As if to add to the causes likely to precipitate guilt, the fact that the fetus may experience pain is becoming more widely recognised. Pain relief is now recommended in pre-term babies undergoing surgery, whereas formerly they were not thought to experience pain and thus not need anaesthesia or analgesia for surgical procedures.[3] That the fetus exhibits a stress response to invasive stimuli is shown by a study from Queen Charlotte's Hospital, London, in which Professor Fisk and his colleagues presented their findings of a hormonal response in the fetal plasma following intrauterine needling.[4]

Since the mechanisms involved in pain perception are not fully understood, a hormonal response cannot be equated at present with the perception of pain. But it is highly suggestive in that a similar hormonal response is mounted by older children and adults to stimuli which they find painful. McCullagh in his impressive study[5] states that it is quite clear that structures

3. K.J.S. Anand et al., 'Randomised Trial of fentanyl anaesthesia in pre-term babies undergoing surgery: effects of the stress response', *Lancet*, 1987, i, 243-7.
4. Giannakoulopoulos, et al., 'Fetal Plasma cortisol and endorphin response to antruteine needling', *Lancet*, vol. 344, 9 July 1994.
5. P. McCullagh, *The Fetus as Transplant Donor* (London, 1987).

responsible for conveying pain impulses to consciousness are likely to be in place and functioning before those capable of inhibiting the sensation of pain. He believes that there is a strong likelihood that the fetus in the first trimester has started to acquire sentient capacity, perhaps as early as six weeks, certainly by nine to ten weeks gestation.

That the post-abortion syndrome exists is now increasingly recognised and is classified as a specific type of post-traumatic stress disorder. Many workers, on the other hand, still regard it as a continuing manifestation of a disturbance already present and that further worsening of the condition is only temporary with no lasting side effects. The evidence presented by the contributors to this volume, however, make it grimly apparent that it does exist and has wide ramifications.

Vincent Rue, who first identified post-abortion trauma as a variant of the post-traumatic stress syndrome in 1981, stresses that denial and numbing is a universal response to truama and is central to the development of the post-abortion syndrome (PAS), because greater amounts of psychic energy are increasingly employed to protect the individual from unwanted and intrusive re-experiencing.

That the assessment of denial or psychogenic numbing plays a dominant role in any methodology is evident from Russell Blacker. In his review of the methodological issue it is evident that the development of new standarised psychiatric instruments and rating scales permits a more reliable analysis of the rates of formal psychiatric disorders than the somewhat impressionistic data obtained from earlier studies. Denial and guilt, together with chaotic and irresponsible life styles, dog research in to PAS. For Blacker the problem is particularly acute in the case of spiritual sequelae such as loss or diminution of faith, unresolved spiritual guilt, reduction in religious activity or altered views of the character and nature of God.

David Larson and John Lyons find that, while objectivity in clinical literature reviews is recognised as an essential characteristic, many reviews fail to meet even minimal standards of scientific credibility. They have developed the systematic review which captures a larger percentage of relevant peer reviewed research studies than standard computerised literature searches. Their examples of selection and interpretation bias in post-abortion research reveal important discrepancies.

Rachel Anderson and David Hanley from the Pine Rest Christian Hospital together with David Larson conducted a study to examine the potential risk factors for long-term abortion-related distress and specifically to assess whether or not women who reported distress from their abortion experience fit a profile consistent with post-traumatic stress disorder, or whether an alternative model of psychological adjustment was warranted. Agneta Sutton finds in the light of the evidence that adverse post-abortion reactions are a widespread phenomenon. It is surely time for health authorities and medical establishments to undertake co-ordinated, international, large-scale studies of the social and psychological consequences of abortion, and indeed review the whole practice of abortion.

Philip Ney deals with the argument that freely available abotion will stop child abuse and neglect. Although a causal relationship between the two has not been proved beyond all reasonable doubt, he presents four studies showing a number of positive correlations. Women who had suffered previous procured abortions were more likely to abuse or neglect their children. In support of this thesis he presents seven compelling arguments.

Margaret White from her vast experience in caring for these mothers presents the clinical situation. Three tragic case studies serve to illustrate the scene. For her it is a rare woman who experiences absolutely no side-effects.

Sandro Findro, as a psychoanalyst, outlines the type of behaviour, the agression and destruction, associated with voluntary termination of pregnancy. But he is not without hope and urges the Christian virtue of repentance.

Patricia Casey, in her contribution, discusses the treatment of the syndrome. Although there is little scientific information on the most appropriate models of intervention in those who suffer from the psychological complications of abortion, those working in this area are advised to use models of treatment used in other forms of bereavement and major trauma.

My grateful thanks are due to Agneta Sutton, on whose inspiration the whole project was based. I am also indebted to Luke Gormally of the Linacre Centre, who corrected my wilder inaccuracies and provided much needed advice. All the contributors were extremely patient as being an international effort much time has been expended on communications.

Post-abortion syndrome: a variant of post-traumatic stress disorder

VINCENT M. RUE

In the mental health community, resistance has all too often been considerable in acknowledging the profound effects of human trauma. This is particularly the case regarding induced abortion. Among mental health practitioners, some are simply unfamiliar with the post-abortion literature. Others are reluctant to examine or affirm post-abortion psychological harm for fear of lending support to a political position in opposition to their own. While others in their clinical practice never 'see' any symptoms of post-abortion trauma because they either do not believe it exists and hence minimize any reported associations with the abortion, or never bother to question the patient about past pregnancy losses and any possible resulting behavioral, cognitive and/or emotional changes.

In general, today, discussion of the emotional sequelae of abortion is perceived as 'politically incorrect' in the US and elsewhere. Any suggestion that abortion can cause significant emotional problems is prone to being discounted and minimised due to the prevailing opinion that abortion only causes relief and maturation.[1] This chapter will focus on some of the existing evidence of post-abortion traumatisation and attempt to provide a limited clinical description of this phenomenon.

ABORTION AND TRAUMA: THE CONTROVERSY

Elective abortion is now the most common surgical procedure in the United States. Existing research on the aftermath of abortion has often yielded

---

1. See for example: American Psychological Association (1987). Research Review: Psychological Sequelae of Abortion. Unpublished testimony presented to the Office of the US Surgeon General. Washington, DC: Author.

contradictory results largely due to methodological shortcomings.[2] There are some 375 studies on the psychological after-effects of induced abortion. Some are anecdotal; some are reviews; and most are so methodologically flawed as to limit their utility. Nevertheless, both sides of the abortion debate refer to various studies suggesting either the existence or non-existence of post-abortion sequelae. One of the chief proponents of abortion's psychological safety, Dr. Henry David, has concluded: 'Regardless of personal convictions about abortion, there is general agreement that uncertainty persists about the psychological sequelae of terminating pregnancies.'[3]

And yet, in a recent assessment of the after-effects of abortion, Adler et al. reported that 'the weight of the evidence in scientific studies indicates that legal abortion of an unwanted pregnancy in the first trimester does not pose a psychological hazard for most women.'[4] Nevertheless, the authors, a panel of experts from the American Psychological Association, acknowledged three confounding problems that severely limit the validity of their own conclusions: 1) 'each study has methodological shortcomings and limitations', 2) 'no definitive conclusions can be drawn about longer-term effects'; and 3) 'women who are more likely to find the abortion experience stressful may be under-represented in volunteer samples.'[5] Even to the most unbiased observer, these limitations would certainly seem to question the validity of making such sweeping claims about the psychological safety of induced abortion at this time.

THE GENESIS OF ABORTION TRAUMA: UNACKNOWLEDGED GRIEF

The essential characteristics of a traumatic event generally include but are not restricted to: 1) a serious threat to one's life; 2) a serious threat to one's physical integrity; 3) a serious threat or possible harm to one's children/spouse/close relative/friends; 4) sudden destruction of one's home/community; 5) seeing another person who has been/is being/has recently been seriously injured or killed; 6) physical violence; and 7) learning about serious threat/harm to relative/family.[6]

When there are physical complications to abortion, a serious threat to one's life is possible. Very often the perceptions of the women feeling

---

2. For a review see A. Speckhard and V. Rue (1992), 'Postabortion Syndrome: An Emerging Public Health Concern', *Journal of Social Issues*, 48, 1992, 95-119.
3. A. David, 'Post Abortion Syndrome?', *Abortion Research Notes* 16:3, December 1987, p. 1.
4. N. Adler et al., 'Psychological Responses After Abortion' *Science*, April 1990, 41-3.
5. Adler et al., pp. 42 and 43.
6. K. Peterson, M. Prout, and R. Schwarz (1991), *Post-Traumatic Stress Disorder: A Clinician's Guide* (New York: Plenum), p. 15.

victimised by their abortion experience includes: 1) the belief that they have killed their child; 2) that the death was violent and unjustified; 3) that the post-abortion feelings of loss and grief were unanticipated; and 4) that their coping abilities post-abortion are overwhelmed. For other women, their abortion trauma becomes manifest only after learning more about fetal development post-abortion or in a subsequent wanted pregnancy. At that point they often describe feeling overwhelmed with sadness, loss and guilt over the death of their fetal child.

When a pregnancy loss such as induced abortion is traumatic, and it cannot be openly acknowledged, publicly mourned or socially supported, the parent lives in isolation. For such an individual, grief is 'disenfranchised.'[7] But there is also an intrapsychic aspect to the sociological reality of disenfranchised grief, namely, self-disenfranchisement.[8] The interaction between society's and the self's disenfranchisement is both cause and effect.

In many cultures, death is an unspeakable loss which generates profound feelings of guilt, shame and grief. Indeed, the defence mechanisms of denial, repression and suppression require and necessitate the maintenance of silence to ward off intrusive feelings of anxiety, pain and stress. It is this same silence that perpetuates self-disenfranchised grief.

According to Kauffman's typology, in self-disenfranchised grief, the individual is responsible for the lack of acknowledgement and acceptance of the painful after-effects of the loss. The primary psychological factor inhibiting the recognition of feelings of grief is shame. One is then disenfranchised by one's own feelings of shame. It is common to feel shame in the face of normal guilt. Shame and its related feelings of alienation and inferiority can be directly attributable to experiences that are defined as 'breaking the interpersonal bridge' as discussed by Kauffman. This occurs when: 1) the familiar becomes foreign; 2) others are de-personalised; 3) there is a failure to act in accordance with internalised concepts of responsibility; 4) internalised values are transgressed; 5) trust is broken down; and 6) stigmatisation and isolation result.[9] Shame and guilt are clearly principal components of traumatisation.[10] If abortion is an intentionally caused human death event, then it is likely that the effects of 'breaking the interpersonal bridge' are considerable and psychologically serious, even traumatic.

When guilt is inhibited, it can lead to complicated mourning. Guilt that

---

7. K. Doka (ed.), *Disenfranchised Grief* (Lexington, Mass: Lexington Books, 1989).
8. J. Kauffman (1989), 'Intrapsychic Dimenions of Disenfranchised Grief,' in K. Doka (ed.), *Disenfranchised Grief* (Lexington, Mass: Lexington Books), 25-42.
9. Ibid., 26-9.
10. M. Wong and D. Cook (1992), 'Shame and Its Contribution to PTSD', *Journal of Traumatic Stress*, 5, 4, 557-62.

is unsanctioned and shame-covered in the mourning process will have consequences commonly associated with guilt complications in impacted and pathological grief, i.e., recurrence of the unresolved guilt produces conflicts in other relationships, fears of abandonment, self-destructive behaviours, anger, feelings of inadequacy, and depression. Ashamed of one's behaviour and emotions, the individual may experience a disorder of one's sense of self, such as emotional numbing, dissociation, self-alienation, and a damaged sense of ego-mastery.[11] These symptoms are characteristic of post-traumatic disorganisation.

Because abortion is an unsanctioned death event, because the decision to terminate the life of one's fetal child is beyond the range of normal human experience, and because abortion can be described as a significant 'breaking of the interpersonal bridge,' individuals experiencing this procedure may commonly condemn themselves to a life of silence and atonement or denial and fear. Unacknowledged grief and guilt, anticipated condemnation by others, as well as the terror of re-experiencing the trauma all enable and maintain the parameters of secrecy and isolation—all characteristic hallmarks of post-traumatic decline. Such an individual becomes 'trauma bonded.'

A CLINICAL EXAMPLE

A 35-year-old woman came for evaluation of post-abortion problems. She had seen numerous therapists, attempted spiritual resolution, attended self-help groups for women hurt from their abortions, and attempted several unsuccessful courses of anti-depressant and hypno-sedative medications. Before her abortion she had experienced several other traumas, including incest and date rape. She was also bulemic. Her abortion experience was traumatic because numerous predisposing risk factors for post-abortion trauma were not evaluated in the counselling she received beforehand. In addition, she attempted to halt the abortion before it was performed, but the doctor did not accede. In her own words:

> I feel like I am falling down a very deep hole, dark and damp, grungy and grimy. The sadness at work is unbearable. I want to grab that baby back and place it inside of me. I feel drained, achy, violated and abused. When I took the sleeping pill, in 20 minutes I started feeling like I did when the doctor gave me Demerol and Valium for the abortion. I started to panic. I felt like I was going out, my legs numbed and I felt unable to control anything. I think when I sleep more feelings surface. Without sleep I stay numb. I feel angry and depressed. The

---

11. Kauffmann (1989), op. cit., p. 27.

tears freely form whenever I am alone . . . they come out from hiding, revealing thoughts I don't yet know I have. But my tears know . . . and they come. They visit at dark, I wonder if they will ever leave.

The Saturdays (day of the abortion two and one half years earlier) of my life hold funeral services for my baby and me. This must explain why I feel numb . . . my legs, my arms, my hands, like my daughter they are appendages and like her they are dead.

It's easier to be into food than it is to acknowledge how I feel. I grieve the loss of my baby and I feel despair because I know I can't bring her back and I know I can't replace her. I fear that my one living child will be taken from me. I cling to my son to somehow hold onto my baby.

I freak when my menstrual blood smears my thighs, hurling me back to the gurney and the abortion. The way I knew my baby was dead was by waking and seeing the blood on my thighs. I fall apart when I see pregnant women. I turn away when I see babies. I change check-out lanes in the supermarket to avoid being too close to them. My abortion was self-destructive. I have intense, uncontrollable anger and rage. I feel barren and I can't forgive myself. I have terrible nightmares of throwing my baby down on the floor in the kitchen. In one dream I chopped off my hair, a vital part of me. I also dreamt that I slit my wrists.

The world keeps the wound alive. I am alive, just half of me, half of us, maybe. I laid on the floor last night for three and a half hours crying, curled up like a fetus.

POST-ABORTION SYNDROME (PAS)

If elective abortion is nothing more than the removal of non-descript cells or tissue, then it would be highly unlikely that such a procedure could cause any significant psychological harm, much less resemble the symptom picture of post-traumatic stress disorder (PTSD). On the other hand, if elective abortion is an intentionally caused human death experience, then it is likely that some women, men and significant others could manifest profound symptoms of intrusion/re-experience, avoidance/denial, associated symptoms, depression, grief and loss. It is also true that stress and trauma begin with one's perception of it. This has certainly been true for the hundreds of women this psychotherapist has treated had been previously unable to recover from their traumatic abortion experiences.

If abortion is experienced as traumatic, the symptomatic responses may be many and varied. They can include: a variety of autonomic, dysphoric and cognitive symptoms; dissociative states lasting from a few minutes to several hours or even days during which components of the abortion are re-lived and the individual behaves as though experiencing the event at the moment; impulsive behaviour, increased irritability, emotional lability, and depression and guilt resulting in self-defeating or suicidal behaviours. Additionally the following may also be seen: emotional distancing and numbing, feelings of helplessness, hopelessness, sadness, sorrow, lowered self-esteem, distrust, hostility toward self and others, regret, sleep disorders, recurring distressing dreams, nightmares, anniversary reactions, psychophysiological symptoms, alcohol and/or chemical dependencies and abuse, sexual dysfunction, insecurity, painful unwanted re-experiencing of the abortion, relationship disruption, communication impairment and/or restriction, isolation, fetal fantasies, self condemnation, flashbacks, uncontrollable weeping, eating disorders, preoccupation, memory and/or concentration disruption, confused and/or distorted thinking, delusions, bitterness, an enduring sense of loss, survivor guilt with an inability to forgive oneself, psychological distress associated with physical complications, and the corresponding increased need for psychotherapeutic and/or psychopharmacological treatment.

Traumatic events have the capability to shatter the individual's core assumptions about reality. In PAS it is common clinically to encounter significant alteration of an individual's primary beliefs of safety, trust, worthiness, meaning in life, pleasure, self image and degree of relatedness/connectedness to others. It is now generally accepted that post-traumatic stress reactions are more persistent after an event for which human beings are perceived to be responsible. Because of this, survivor guilt, shame and a chronic inability to forgive oneself and the need to punish are commonly found impediments to recovery. There is also evidence that an individual experiencing an abortion is more likely to be traumatised if she believes that the procedure is *absolutely safe* psychologically. Events need to be given meaning before they are experienced as stressful or not.[12]

PAS defined as PTSD

In 1987, the American Psychiatric Association acknowledged in its newly revised manual of diagnostic criteria, the *Diagnostic and Statistical Manual of Mental Disorders III-R* (DSM-III-R), that abortion is a type of 'psychosocial stressor.' Psychological stressors are capable of causing 'post-traumatic stress disorder.' Post-abortion Syndrome is a specific type of post-traumatic stress disorder. As a psychological disorder, PAS is made up of a predictable pattern of symptoms which occur in response to a physically or emotionally traumatising abortion experience. Impairment from the disorder may either

---

12. See generally: Peterson, Prout & Schwarz (1991) op. cit., p. 117.

be mild or affect nearly every aspect of life. 'Psychic numbing' may interfere with interpersonal relationships, such as marriage or family life. Depression and guilt may result in self-defeating behaviour or suicidal actions. Drug or alcohol abuse may develop and 'anniversary reactions' are common. Increased irritability and impulsive behaviour are also associated features of this disorder.[13]

According to the DSM-III-R, post-traumatic stress disorder traumata involve 'an event that is outside the range of usual human experience . . . e.g. serious threat to one's life or physical integrity; serious threat or harm to one's children . . . or seeing another person who has been or is being, seriously injured or killed as the result of . . . physical violence.' (p. 250) There are four basic components of PAS: 1) exposure to or participation in an abortion experience, i.e., the intentional destruction of one's unborn child, which is perceived as sufficiently traumatic and beyond the range of usual human experience; 2) uncontrolled negative re-experiencing of the abortion death event, e.g. flashbacks, nightmares, grief and anniversary reactions; 3) unsuccessful attempts to avoid or deny abortion recollections and emotional pain which result in reduced responsiveness with others and one's environment; and 4) experiencing associated symptoms not present before the abortion including guilt about surviving.[14]

Women with PAS experience feelings of alienation, isolation and horror over having experienced an abortion. For many, this death event is sufficiently traumatic and beyond the range of human experience so as to be re-experienced and the cause of impacted grieving. Some of the fears experienced include: fears about what happened to the aborted child, fears about one's own body, fears about one's sanity, fears about one's spiritual standing, and fears about being socially ostracised or branded as a deviant should others learn about the abortion.

The diagnostic criteria for PAS are provided in Figure 1. Spontaneous recovery from PAS is not characteristic. While PAS is categorised as a type of PTSD, additional diagnoses including anxiety, depressive or organic mental disorder may concurrently be made. Other variants of PTSD, not dissimilar to PAS, are 'Rape Trauma Syndrome,' 'Battered Wives' Syndrome,' and 'Post-Hysterectomy Syndrome,' all of which are also not included in the DSM-III-R, but which are widely accepted.

More than an accidental grab bag of isolated symptoms, Post-abortion

---

13. V. Rue and A. Speckhard (1992), 'Post Abortion Trauma: Incidence and Diagnostic Considerations,' *Medicine and Mind*, 6, 1, 57-74.
14. See also A. Speckhard and V. Rue (1992), 'Postabortion Syndrome: An Emerging Public Health Concern,' *Journal of Social Issues*, 48, 95-120; A. Speckhard and V. Rue (1993), 'Complicated Mourning: Dynamics of Impacted Post-Abortion Grief,' *Journal of Pre- and Peri-natal Psychology*, 8, 1, 6-32.

Syndrome is a clustering of related and unsuccessful attempts to assimilate and gain mastery over the abortion trauma. The resulting lifestyle changes involve partial to total cognitive restructuring, behavioural reorganisation, and emotional disruption.

Characteristic symptoms: intrusion/re-experience and avoidance/denial

Women who are emotionally traumatised by their abortions, and perhaps physically traumatised as well, are frequently overwhelmed by the depths of emotions that the abortion experience evokes. The factors of being surprised and overwhelmed by the intensity of the emotional and physical response to the abortion experience frequently act upon the post-abortive woman in a manner which causes her to resort to the defences of repression and denial. The woman who represses or denies her emotional responses to the abortion trauma often re-experiences that trauma in memory at a later time. It is generally true that the PTSD symptom picture, particularly a person who experienced a traumatic abortion, worsens as the magnitude of the trauma rises, as the chronicity of the disorder increases, and as the delay in treatment lengthens.[15]

In the case of PAS, re-experience can occur in women who frequently experience nightmares following their abortion. One woman reported a recurring nightmare in which she dreams that her aborted baby is drowning in a swimming pool and she desperately and unsuccessfully keeps reaching out to save the child. Another woman described her nightly horror of wakening in a panic hearing the desperate crying of a newborn in a nightmare and then searching the house in vain to find the infant.

Re-experience also occurs in PAS women in the form of preoccupation in their waking and sleeping moments with thoughts about pregnancy in general, and the aborted child in particular. Such preoccupation frequently becomes most intense on subsequent anniversary dates of the abortion or on anniversaries of the projected due date of the aborted child. One woman described her monthly re-experiencing around her menses. During her menstruation, this married woman would ritually go into her bathroom and take a glass bottle to capture any blood clots in the hope of capturing any remnants of her two year old abortion.

PAS re-experience also occurs in the form of flashbacks to the abortion experience. As one woman described her flashbacks, 'I keep hearing the sickening suction machine. It just goes off in my head and I can't stop it.' Others avoid pregnant women, medical clinics, or babies for fear of flashing back to their traumatic loss.

15. See, generally, C. Frederick (1980), 'Effects of natural versus human-induced violence upon victims', *Evaluation and Change* (special issue), 71-5.

According to Klein, three out of four people surveyed keep sexual secrets, like abortion, from their partners and even sometimes from themselves.[16] By not acknowledging an abortion experience to one's self and/or to one's significant others, a psychological barrier is erected and an emotional toxicity is perpetuated. Coupled with denial, avoidance of abortion-related traumata can occur on a number of levels: 1) avoidance of affect/feelings (numbing); 2) avoidance of knowledge of the event (amnesia); 3) behavioral avoidance (phobic responses); and 4) avoidance of communication about the event (interpersonal distancing).[17]

When intrusion and re-experience of the trauma become too threatening, the defences of avoidance and denial help restore some sense of balance and mastery rather than feeling overwhelmed. Accordingly, affect is protected and limited coping mechanisms are restored. Confronting traumatic memories may pose a seemingly unresolvable discrepancy with the individual's existing schemas about the self and the world.[18] This may be particularly so in abortion because denial functions as a protective mechanism against experiencing the grief and loss surrounding the abortion death. One woman, when asked how she coped with her abortion experience replied: 'I didn't take it personally.' Although clinical experiences indicate that denial/numbing is a universal response to trauma, denial is also central to the development of PAS because greater amounts of psychic energy are increasingly employed to protect the individual from unwanted and intrusive re-experiencing.

Various types of denial have been described by Rue relating to abortion: occluded, periodic, compensatory, segmented, and purposive.[19] Selby delineated abortion denial according to stages: 1) preabortion denial (a) of the pregnancy itself; (b) of the responsibility for the pregnancy; (c) of the baby or humanity of the product of conception; or (d) of how she became pregnant; 2) during the abortion event denial (a) of the physical experience itself; (b) of her emotional reactions to the procedure; and 3) post-abortion denial (a) of certain aspects of the abortion; (b) of all memory of the abortion; and (c) of any relationship between the abortion and self-defeating behaviours.[20] To the extent that denial is intractable, recovery is minimised.

---

16. M. Klein (1987), 'Sexual Secrets', paper presented at the annual meeting of the Society for the Scientific Study of Sex, Beverly Hills, CA.
17. See generally K. Peterson, M. Prout and R. Schwarz (1991), *Post-Traumatic Stress Disorder: A Clinician's Guide* (New York: Plenum Press).
18. I. McCann and L. Pearlman (1990), *Psychological Trauma and the Adult Survivor* (New York: Brunner/Mazel).
19. V. Rue (1986), 'Post-Abortion Syndrome', paper presented at the 1st National Conference on Post-Abortion Healing, University of Notre Dame.
20. T. Selby (1990), *The Mourning After: Help for Post-Abortion Syndrome* (Grand Rapids, Michigan: Baker).

Women with PAS may employ repression in an attempt to 'forget' parts or the whole of the abortion trauma, creating 'psychogenic amnesia' which is a central feature of PTSD. This memory loss may be temporary or chronic. The tendency to avoid dealing with a traumatic abortion experience must be overcome for three reasons: (1) patients cannot process the traumatic experience if they avoid everything about it and hence are held 'hostage;' (2) the avoidance/denial itself becomes a secondary problem that further exacerbates the situation; and (3) the likelihood of future mastery of potentially highly stressful events is diminished considerably with unresolved past trauma.

When a woman's experience of an abortion trauma is delayed, it can cause confusion, fear, and bewilderment in the woman who thought she had successfully dealt with her abortion experience. One woman spoke of it this way, 'I can't believe it's my abortion that's bothering me after all these years. It was okay at the time, but now I feel really upset about it and afraid to be alone with my feelings.'

CORROBORATING EVIDENCE

Post-abortion trauma was first identified as a variant of post-traumatic stress disorder in 1981 by Rue.[21] Subsequently, additional clinicians/researchers have confirmed this diagnostic impression: Stanford-Rue, 1986;[22] Speckhard, 1987;[23] Fisch & Tadmor (1989),[24] Selby (1990),[25] DeVeber & Azenstat (1991),[26] and Angelo (1992).[27]

In a very recent study of 984 women randomly selected for follow-back from their abortion, Barnard found approximately 60 per cent gave a wrong phone number at the abortion clinic. Because of this, she was only able to obtain a sample of 80 women. Nevertheless, her findings are important: (1) 68 per cent, at the time of the abortion had little to no religious involvement;

---

21. V. Rue (1981), 'Abortion and Family Relations', testimony presented before the Subcommittee on the Constitution of the US Senate Judiciary Committee, US Senate, 97th Congress, Washington, DC.
22. S. Stanford-Rue (1986), *Will I Cry Tomorrow? Healing Post-Abortion Trauma* (Fleming, NJ: Revell).
23. A. Speckhard (1987), *Psycho-Social Stress Following Abortion*, (Kansas City, MO: Sheed & Ward).
24. R. Fisch and O. Tadmor (1989), 'Iatrogenic Post-Traumatic Stress Disorder', *Lancet*, 9 December 1397.
25. T. Selby (1990), *The Mourning After*, op. cit.
26. L. DeVeber, J. Azenstat and D. Chisholm (1991), 'Postabortion Grief: Psychological Sequelae of Induced Abortion', *Humane Medicine*, 7, 203-9.
27. E.J. Angelo (1992), 'Psychiatric Sequelae of Abortion: The Many Faces of Post-Abortion Grief', *Linacre Quarterly*, 59, 2, 69-80.

(2) the sample was normally distributed as to values; (3) 3-5 years post abortion, 18 per cent of the sample met the full diagnostic criteria for post-traumatic stress disorder and 46 per cent displayed high stress reactions (symptoms of intrusion and avoidance) to their abortion. Barnard used standardised psychological testing, including the Millon Clinical Multiaxial Inventory and the Impact of Event Scale. She found approximately one out of four women reported feeling emotionally detached and numb and more than one out of three described conscious efforts to avoid thinking about their abortion experience. More than one out of three identified difficulties of increased unwanted and negative arousal patterns from their abortion experience, including hypervigilence, sleep disorders, and startle reactions.[28]

In a carefully designed recent study, Hanley, Piersma, King, Larson & Foy evaluated whether some women in outpatient mental health treatment with a presenting problem of postabortion distress met DSM-III-R criteria for the Post-traumatic Stress Disorder (PTSD) categories of intrusion, avoidance, and hyperarousal. One hundred and five women were administered the SCID-PTSD module, the Impact of Event Scale, as well as the Social Support Questionnaire and the Interview for Recent Life Events, in addition to completing a semi-structured interview. The researchers concluded: 'the data from this study are suggestive that women can report abortion-related distress similar to classic PTSD symptoms of intrusion, avoidance and hyperarousal and that these symptoms can be present many years after the abortion.'[29]

Using a large probability sample of 957 women, Miller asked women who were at a minimum of 60 days post-abortion how they felt. He found: 22 per cent reported they felt worse, describing a feeling of 'sexlessness' or feeling out of touch with their body, at two weeks post-abortion, 38 per cent indicated that they felt relief mixed with feelings of distress with 18 per cent indicating they felt distress only; and 22 per cent reported some significant emotional upset or disturbance after the first few post-abortion weeks.[30] Even more important than these findings, Miller's research has provided preliminary empirical support for the theoretical modeling of pre-abortion decision making and post-abortion loss from a trauma perspective.

28. C. Barnard, *The Long Term Psychosocial Effects of Abortion*, Portsmouth, N.H.: Institute for Abortion Recovery and Research, 1990.
29. D. Hanley, H. Piersma, D. King, D. Larson and D. Foy (23 October 1992), 'Women outpatients reporting continuing post-abortion distress: A preliminary inquiry', paper presented at the Eighth Annual Meeting of the International Society for Traumatic Stress Studies, Los Angeles.
30. W. Miller (1992), 'An empirical study of the psychological antecedents and consequences of induced abortion', *Journal of Social Issues*, 48, 67-94.

For a more comprehensive review of the literature and the documentation of other types of psychological injury post-abortion, the reader is referred to Rue (1994) and Speckhard & Rue (1992).[31]

CONCLUSION

While the post-abortion debate has generated considerable controversy, according to Wilmoth: 'There is now virtually no disagreement among researchers that some women experience negative psychological reactions post-abortion.'[32] For women who have elected abortion, the volitional nature of their loss may place them at special risk for traumatisation as opposed to women who experienced stillbirth or miscarriage, over which they had no control.

In the emotionally charged public debate about abortion, overstatements abound. Some claim abortion is psychologically devastating to most.[33] Others claim that there is no evidence whatsoever of any post-abortion trauma.[34] Given the methodological weaknesses in the existing literature, the diversity of studies available, and the weight of consistent clinical evidence, any public pronouncements concerning the psychological safety of induced abortion are at this time premature at best, and at worst, misleading and harmful to women's health.

With improved research that would include large sample size, comparison groups, and differential gender responses, a more accurate assessment would be possible. Rhetoric aside, honest scientific and clinical discourse converges and confirms that there are women and men who are psychologically traumatised from their abortion experiences and that for some, their clinical profile may best be described as a type of post-traumatic stress disorder. These individuals need compassion, understanding, and genuine assistance, not judgment, disbelief and stigmatisation. Only then will women and men be encouraged to seek treatment and recovery from such a traumatic event that was entirely unanticipated.

---

31. V. Rue (1994), 'The Psychological Realities of Induced Abortion,' in Mannion, M. (ed.), *Post-Abotion Aftermath: A Comprehensive Consideration* (Kansas City, Sheed & Ward), in press. A. Speckhard and V. Rue (1992) see note 14.
32. G. Wilmoth (1992), 'Abortion, Public Health Policy, and Informed Consent Legislation', *Journal of Social Issues*, 48, 3, 1-17, 5.
33. Nancyjo Mann in D. Reardon (1987), *Aborted Women: Silent No More* (Westchester, Ill: Crossway), p. xxiv.
34. N. Stotland (1992). 'The Myth of the Abortion Trauma Syndrome', *Journal of the American Medical Association*, 268, 15, 2078-9.

Figure 1: Post-Abortion Syndrome: Diagnostic Criteria

A. *Stressor:* The abortion experience, i.e., the intentional destruction of one's unborn child, is sufficiently traumatic and beyond the range of usual human experience so as to cause significant symptoms of re-experience, avoidance, and impacted grieving.

B. *Re-experience:* The abortion trauma is re-experienced in one of the following ways:

1. recurrent and intrusive distressing recollections of the abortion experience;
2. recurrent distressing dreams of the abortion or of the unborn child (e.g., baby dreams or fetal fantasies);
3. sudden acting or feeling as if the abortion were recurring (including reliving the experience, illusions, hallucinations, and dissociative (flashback) episodes including upon awakening or when intoxicated);
4. intense psychological distress at exposure to events that symbolise or resemble the abortion experience (e.g., medical clinics, pregnant mothers, subsequent pregnancies, menstruation, or sexual intercourse) including anniversary reactions of intense grieving and/or depression on subsequent anniversary dates of the abortion or on the projected due date of the aborted child.

C. *Avoidance:* Persistent avoidance of stimuli associated with the abortion trauma or numbing of general responsiveness (not present before the abortion), as indicated by at least three of the following:

1. efforts to avoid or deny thoughts or feelings associated with the abortion;
2. efforts to avoid activities, situations, or information that might arouse recollections of the abortion (e.g., pregnant women, infants, etc.);
3. inability to recall the abortion experience or an important aspect of the abortion (psychogenic amnesia);
4. markedly diminished interest in significant activities;
5. feeling of detachment or estrangement from others, including withdrawal in relationships and/or reduced communication;
6. restricted range of affect (e.g. unable to have loving or tender feelings and/or diminished sexual libido);
7. sense of foreshortened future, e.g., does not expect to have a career, marriage, or children, or a long life.

D. *Associated features:* Persistent symptoms (not present before the abortion), as indicated by at least two of the following:

1. difficulty falling or staying asleep;
2. irritability or outbursts of anger;
3. difficulty concentrating;
4. hyper-vigilence;
5. exaggerated startle response to intrusive recollections or re- experiencing of the abortion trauma;
6. physiologic reactivity upon exposure to events or situations that symbolize or resemble an aspect of the abortion (e.g., breaking out in a profuse sweat upon a pelvic examination or hearing vacuum pump sounds);
7. depression and suicidal ideation;
8. guilt about surviving when one's unborn child did not;
9. self devaluation and/or an inability to forgive one's self;
10. secondary substance abuse;
11. eating disorders.

E. *Course:* Duration of the disturbance (symptoms in B, C, and D) of more than one month's duration, or onset may be delayed (greater than six months after the abortion).

Note: Developed by Vincent M. Rue, from diagnostic criteria for 'post traumatic stress disorder' in the *Diagnostic and Statistical Manual of Mental Disorders III-R* (DSM-III-R), American Psychiatric Association, (1989, p. 250-1). The American Psychiatric Association in no way supports the existence of, nor does it find any clinical evidence for the basis of the diagnosis of 'post abortion syndrome.' The *DSM-III-R* does not reference nor include the diagnosis of 'post abortion syndrome' at this time. However, the *DSM-III-R* does list abortion as a 'psychosocial stressor'.

Post-abortion syndrome

SANDRO GINDRO

I

Abortion (from the Latin, *aboriri*, to die), or interruption of pregnancy, as many somewhat hyprocritically prefer to say, to lighten its grim meaning, when performed voluntarily, may be looked at from two different points of view—that of nature and that of morality. If no pathological conditions interrupt the process, pregnancy tends by nature to take its course and end with birth. Thus any more or less violent termination of that process must be considered unnatural. However, one must be careful not to use the concept of nature in a too dogmatic and undiscriminating way.

What is nature? Is nature the physical, biological, animal, vegetable and mineral world? Does it mean the essence of an existing thing? What is meant when something is described as 'natural'? Many people attribute two different overlapping meanings to the word 'natural'. On the one hand, it is taken as meaning something which takes place in line with established metaphysical laws; on the other, as something spontaneous and unimpeded. In the opinion of many, nature coincides with 'good *par excellence*', whereas anything absolutely evil would be considered unnatural. Unnatural behaviour violates the laws of some unfathomable, though not necessarily divine, design, which transcends the will of the individual. That which is genuine and not artificial, not manipulated, and, therefore, in some sense pure, is considered natural? They say that 'Nature must follows its course'. But what is the course of nature?

Nature meets and defies man's desire. Desire may accord with nature, but it may also, quite rightly, seek to alter it, if some aspect of it is deemed undesirable. If that were not so, medicine and, more generally, any form of therapy should be condemned as unnatural and wrong. To replace a removed organ with an artificial one would go against nature, which does not provide for the possibility of growing new organs. Indeed, it if were unnatural to alter anything in nature, the legitimacy of the use of crutches or wheelchairs should be questioned. For, would it not be more natural to use only a stick broken from a tree? According to the argument that all alterations of things natural are unnatural, transplants are unnatural and so too is wine-making and cooking and any pharmacology that is not Galenic. Natural man should quench his thirst at springs, using his hands as a cup. He should satisfy his appetite with wild fruits. Pursuing this line of reasoning to its ultimate conclusion, it would follow that it is unnatural to build houses to live in as well as to use transport such as trains, cars and aeroplanes, and navigation should be limited to the use of floating tree-trunks. The laws of nature have often been invoked to uphold strange theories. The behaviour of a political enemy may be judged unnatural, as may, from the point of view of religion, that of a somewhat unorthodox person. In fact, human life, regarded in this way, would be described as an uninterrupted sequence of unnatural acts, contrary to the 'natural' or 'inborn' flux of events. Radically, only God has a right to intervene in the running of things—though, he may do so even if his intervention involves the destruction of universal order, including the genetic pattern of the human species.

In reality, nature is bent by man for reasons of desire and pleasure. It is natural to give in to desire. The question is, to which pleasures, and whose, we should give in? To all living beings? To the majority? One answer is that of the Italian, Cesare Beccaria, who wrote, in 1764, in his work *Dei delitti e delle pene* (On Crime and Punishment), that our aim must be 'the maximum happiness for the majority of people' (*Beccaria*–3), a formulation that utilitarians such as Jeremy Bentham and John Stuart Mill later made their own. In fact, the principle of utilitarianism has always guided human behaviour. It did so even before it was developed into a system of philosophy in England. For the seventeenth- and eighteenth-century utilitarian the ultimate good consisted in the achievement, on behalf of society, of happiness for the biggest possible number of people. This philosophy is not without merit. Perhaps that is the very reason why subsequent philosophers have persistently tried to prove the utilitarian principle wrong and impractical. Suffice it to say here that the utilitarian principle has guided the behaviour of societies which have wanted to give themselves some form of collective moral philosophy. Crusades, wars and revolutions have been declared, carried out and fought in the name of man's well-being in this life and the next. Obviously it has always been a question of making more or less vast groups happy, given the objective impossibility of finding valid universal parameters. Only occasional delirious minds have claimed that the good to be sought and achieved should be their own, or that of the entire world. Man has always been seeking happiness through pleasure shared with others. The search for pleasure is, therefore, natural and even sacrosanct; it should not create fear. Nature in general, and human nature is particular, is orientated towards pleasure, and this should be admitted without embarrassment or false modesty. Too many crimes have been committed because people think they can ignore this truth, while coining arbitrary concepts of what is natural and labelling certain behaviours unnatural with a cry of 'God wishes it to be so!'

Moral philosophy and nature both demands absolute respect for life in all its forms. Any voluntary interruption of pregnancy is therefore immoral and unnatural; it means the suppression of a life which has the same right to be respected as any other. This is true if the future life in question would be one full of pain both for the person himself and for his surrounding. Any conceptual attempt to justify some form of murder is unnatural and immoral. Murder is never justified, if it were, nobody would be allowed to live unless he could prove that he was destined to become an Arian adult, happy and healthy, in mind and body, and capable of making others happy. In particular, it should be emphasised that even the fruits of rape and violence have a right to life. Killing the embryo does not alter the reality of what has happened but only adds to one wrong another irreparable crime. The small agglomerate of cells originating from the union of the two gametes must be respected; it is already a human being like any other person. An embryo, a foetus, a baby and an archbishop, all have the same right to life.

As to the objections of those who think of the uterus as a hotel, owned by the woman, it should be said that—however absurd this may sound—from the time of conception, the woman must give up any claim to ownership. From that time onwards, the uterus serves to fulfil a social responsibility. The purpose of the maternal womb is to host and protect the fruit of the two gametes which met there, the new human being, until it is capable of life outside the uterus. At that precise moment, the woman's total ownership of her womb ceases, as does her freedom of self-determination. In fact, for the woman, conception means expropriation of her uterus by a new life, whether it be the fruit of a voluntary act or that of an imposition. Modern reproductive techniques prove clearly enough that the function of the uterus is that of hosting. And, there are various ways of hiring its services. One woman may, as a gesture of love, offer her own uterus to her daughter for implantation of a fertilised oocyte, which her daughter cannot herself gestate. Another woman may offer the same services for money. This shows the uterus is in some respects separate from the woman's body—the integrity of which must, nevertheless, be respected. There are many ways of selling one's body, some legal and respectable, some not. Whichever way a woman goes about letting her womb to another, the being housed by the uterus has its own inalienable rights, the first of which is the right to life. It is a human being; nobody can pretend to own it. Not even the symbiotic relationship of pregnancy can provide a dispensation from the obligation to show respect for another life. Rather, it calls for love, mutual love. Indeed, it is tragic when the two lives, that of the mother and that of the child, cannot coexist in harmony, but one life exists against the will of the other.

For the sake of the life that she is hosting, the woman has the right to every form of protection of her own body and person as well as to maximum comfort. In exchange she is answerable to society for the safety of the embryo and foetus until the moment of birth. The course of history, by virtue of which we have come to recognise the principle of the 'sanctity of human life', cannot be changed. The destruction of a single human life generates further violence.

II

Does post-abortion syndrome—a complex of different symptoms due to certain specific causes—exist? If so, is it possible to do anything about it? If abortion is viewed as intentional murder, the guilt that results from it may be understood as a form of expiation. And, without expiation there is no possibility of healing and redemption—or so Socratic wisdom has it, as we are shown by Plato in chapter 35 of the dialogue known as *Gorgias*. To quote from this dialogue:

> *Socrates:* It appears, does it not, that the greatest evil of all is injustice and the committing of unjust acts?
> *Polos:* Of course.
> *Socrates:* And freeing oneself form such evil consists in paying—in the name of justice—the debts incurred by one's guilt?
> *Polos:* In the end that's right!
> *Socrates:* While it has been proved that evading the punishment means prolonging the evil?
> *Polos:* Yes.
> *Socrates:* It follows, therefore, that committing a crime is the minor evil and comes in second place; the greatest intrinsic evil of all is that of evading punishment when guilty.

But would it make sense to talk about post-abortion syndrome, if it were accepted that a woman, or society, may really have legitimate grounds for killing a foetus or an embryo. Experience shows that after an abortion there is always a degree of unease, felt not only by the mother but also by her surroundings, regardless of the political or cultural context of the event. Some people regard this is as a consequence of the moral and religious disapproval expressed by certain sections of society, fostering feelings of guilt, without which there would be no basis for post-abortion syndrome. Without this disapproval, reasons for guilt would be missing—as, in fact, they are in the case of most behaviour condemned by current moral philosophies. Temi, the ancient Greek goddess, is the guarantor of the natural moral order (cf. K. Kerenyi, *Die Mythologie der Griechen*, 1963; Ital. trans., Milan, 1978, pp. 96-7).

III

In the last twenty years of my professional life as a psychoanalyst, I have obviously had many women patients who have experienced one or more abortions. Also, my work as a supervisor of other psychoanalysts, working at the school I have founded, has widened my experience in this area. As may be expected, the number of this kind of patient has risen in recent years. And I can confirm that I have never come across a woman who has been through this distressing experience without suffering from significant psychological consequences. I shall now refer to two cases which I consider significant.

Case 1

Not long ago I was visited by a 66-year-old woman, who was marreid with four children, two boys and two girls—and a large number of grandchildren. She was from the country, not particularly well educated but very pious and active. She had an apparently healthy life behind her, both physically and mentally, which she had passed in relative comfort.

Some months before we met, she had begun to feel rheumatic pains, not particularly acute but nevertheless disturbing. They had made her fall into a state of deep frustration. She had begun to feel old, and to tell herself so repeatedly, so much so that she actually became less independent. She tried to face the problem through unsatisfying pilgrimages to various medical specialists who prescribed medicines and cures that she refused to take. Her anxiety seemed to express itself in frantic consultations with one specialist after another in different towns—much to her family's desperation. She was completely absorbed in her search for the next possible doctor; she talked to her friends about it; she read newspapers and magazines; and she watched to television programmes.

At one point she felt in better spirits, willing to accept, as she said, the cross 'which the Lord has sent me'. She returned to a fairly active life, but this lasted only for a few weeks. Suddenly, one Easter morning she felt incapable of getting out of bed. She didn't go to church, committing thus what she felt was a grave sin. She didn't take part in the traditional family lunch. She felt oppressed by an unceasing tiredness and she had terrible stomach pains. She was left alone, spending the day in her big bedroom, sleeping in darkness and silence. This went on for several days; she was in a state of total depression. She refused to get up, eat, wash herself or do anything. She cried constantly and the doctor gave her some light drugs which seemed to relieve her, but only for a short time. She then fell back into a state of depression combined with a state of confusion. Sometimes she did not recognise her husband or her children. She confused her dreams with reality, the present with the past. She spoke of times long past and then remained silent for long periods.

She was brought to me against her will. But after the first diffident moments, she let herself go and started to speak with a strong local accent, ignoring me completely, as if she was unsure that I was present. I saw her several days in a row. She alternated between diffidence and a desire to speak. I began to go over her medical records. She was shocked when I asked her if she had ever consulted magicians, holy men, pranotherapists or anything 'alternative'. She looked at me severely and said, 'I don't want to commit that sin too! I'm already suffering too much.' Following this, the story of an abortion came slowly to light.

She had decided to resort to an abortion when, at the age of nineteen and pregnant by the man who was to become her husband, she decided that she could not go through with 'such a scandalous pregnancy' (no marriage plans had yet been announced). Despite the sadness of the event for both of them—although it was, as she called it, a 'healthy' decision—it would appear that, as time passed, she got over it.

She said, 'I had repented, my confessor had absolved me; my life could have continued peacefully. I was fine. I tried to be an honest mother for my children later on, even if I was a bit strict. Perhaps, I didn't love them enough. I loved my husband very much and I still feel very tied to him.'

The Good Friday before her dramatic attack she had thought for a moment that her rheumatic pains might be Divine punishment for that ancient sin of her youth, which deep down she had perceived as a crime.

Case 2

One day I found myself before a 25-year-old girl, who had come to me on her own initiative. She faced me defiantly. She worked in a job which, even nowadays in our culture, is considered a masculine prerogative. She spoke quickly and decisively. She told me her story without apparent embarrassment.

'I haven't been able to sleep for three months', she said, 'I eat and I feel sick, I am constantly arguing with my husband, my mother, my in-laws and my brother. What upsets me most, however—and the reason I have come to see you—is the fact that I am treating my three-year-old boy badly. Yet, I love him and I do not want to hurt him. I must be cured straight away, because I fear that I am on the edge of madness. I have terrible dreams, which afterwards I cannot remember. I wake up suddenly and I switch on the light. I often sleep with the light on. I shiver and I am cold. I am off sick at work. I feel as if I am going mad and I cannot bear making my little boy suffer any more. He has seen me change and I feel myself that I have changed. If in the past I felt very little pleasure from making love with my husband, now I feel none at all. In fact, I find it physically revolting. I feel that he is far away from me—that everybody is. I have the feeling that at any moment some terrible disaster is going to happen to me. I sense a catastrophe around the corner and I am afraid of going out by myself.

I asked her when this feeling of unease had begun and if she could connect it with anything that had happened.

'Perhaps it coincided with a serious case of food poisoning that I had from seafood. It was summer and I was very ill. I have never recovered.'

She began to let her imagination run away with her, suggesting that certain poisons might have remained in her body and might be destroying her brain cells. Despite her great fear, her attitude remained defiant and aggressive. After a long silence she suddenly said to me:

'Yes, something did happen which you might think is connected with all this. But I can assure you that it had nothing to do with it. I am sure it is in no way connected! A month before I fell ill I had an abortion, because we could not afford a second child. My husband had some doubts about it. But I am convinced that it is the woman's choice. She alone has the right to make. Isn't that so?'

Her penetrating look, full of cold fury and at the same time desperate, almost pierced me.

'Of course, I was frightened, and that might have affected me. But it was only fear of the operation. Apart from that, I can assure that I had no doubts, hesitations or regrets. Abortion is legal; it is a right to resort to it when necessary. There is no reason to feel guilty. It is not a crime!'

Once again her terrible looks struck me like lightning. Throughout the time she was in my care, she went on repeating to me, almost like a prayer, in between the tales of her everyday life, dreams and thoughts: 'That is right, is it not, Doctor? It cannot be a sin, if it is legal . . .'. I did not want to say anything, I tried to make her speak about other things. I asked her to tell me about her dreams. One day her husband phoned me to say that Laura was not going to continue with her analysis because I had not helped her enough.

These two clinical cases speak for themselves. I am now pursuing further studies of post-abortion syndrome with the help of the other psychosociologists at our psychoanalitical institute for social research. Our studies are not confined to psychoanalitical patients. My experiences so far confirm the fact that women always experience deep unease after an abortion; subsequently often accompanied by aggression and violence towards their children, husbands and pets, and sometimes also expressing itself in some form of self-destruction. The fact that abortion, once illegal, now is legal and regarded as medical treatment has changed virtually nothing. Abortion is a kind of social pathology linked to the administration of violence nad death.

IV

I have pointed to two types of behaviour closely connected with voluntary termination of pregnancy. Both express great aggression and destruction. One seeks punishment through the display of, sometimes quite serious organic symptoms, partly betraying a perception, even if obscure, of the reasons for the sought punishment. The other is an almost maniacal refusal of any responsibility, expressing itself as a complete intolerance of any form of criticism from anybody. In both cases the personality of the patient changes and she becomes strongly paranoid, with delusions of grandeur and illusions of powers. The close contact with the death of a being, whom most cultures and the 'social unconscious' (or our social conscience) teach is an integral part of the maternal body, leaves indelible marks. Undoubtedly, not only the details of each personal story contribute to this phenomenon: the woman's personality and the verdict of the 'social unconscious' also play their part. In addition, the event sets in motion an obscure mechanism, which I call the 'instinctive unconscious' and which rebels against such close contact with death. The fantasies of power-seeking to compensate for this phenomenon hardly ever manage to provide enough reassurance. It may well be that post-abortion syndrome, insofar as it exists, actually has its roots in this 'instinctive unconscious'.

I would not want my discussion to conclude without a glimmer of hope. One woman coming to me with all her anger, said, 'I know you are against abortion. That is precisely why I am asking you to help me. After my third abortion, I collapsed mentally. I no longer have peace. I want to destroy myself. I am not seeking pity. I want to understand what is happening and to rid myself of the experience of death within me'. The therapist must always try to help people to get over suffering; this, then, is my honest task. And so let me remind you of the words: 'Woman, where are those thine accusers? Hath no man condemned thee?' She said, 'No man, Lord'—And Jesus said unto her: 'Neither do I condemn thee; Go, and sin no more'.

It may be noted that I have discussed the question of conflict in terms of two different systems of morals, both of great value. The former belongs to the man Socrates, the latter belongs to the Lord Jesus.

Christian morality does not coincide with the Socratic one, to which I referred in the first pages. Socrates spoke of the importance of expiation, although he held that it would be better not to commit the sin at all. But if the sin has already been committed, it would be an even greater sin to fail to observe the principles of justice and truth and seek to avoid expiation through punishment. According to Socrates, expiation serves to re-establish the broken balance and heal the soul which has been marked by guilt.

Abortion is a crime, crying out to God and man for revenge. God has the right to punish. And so may man, who has given himself laws entailing punishment for crime.

In the Gospel, Jesus speaks a language which, perhaps, none of us today is fully able to understand. He does not speak of punishment by others but urges the adulteress not to sin again. Perhaps, the worst 'punishment' we can get comes from within ourselves and hence it is possible that sin can be expiated only by repenting. The justice of mankind, however, which must also be administrated, is confined to other means.

Crime must not be denied; it must be punished. But we should remember the words: 'He that is without sin among you, let him cast the first stone'.

Selected and interpretation bias in post-abortion research

MARY A. GREENWOLD, DAVID B. LARSON,
JOHN S. LYONS, KIMBERLEY A. SHERRILL

INTRODUCTION

While objectivity in clinical literature reviews is recognised as an essential characteristic, many reviews fail to meet even minimal standards of scientific credibility. For example, as recently as 1987, Mulrow showed that among a group of 50 clinical reviews, only one had clearly specified methods of identifying, selecting, and validating included information.

The systematic review (SR) is one approach to improving the objectivity of reviews. In psychiatry, SRs have been used to assess the quantity and quality of research in areas of clinical controversy, particularly those which have been insufficiently or inadequately studied (Larson et al., 1986; Larson et al., 1988; Larson et al., 1992a, Sherrill et al., 1993). Systematic reviews differ from traditional approaches in that they utilise quantitative methods not only in the selection of articles, but also in the interpretation of the articles (Larson et al., 1986; Larson et al., 1992a; Larson et al., 1992b; Larson et al., 1994).

Systematic reviews also capture a larger percentage of relevant peer reviewed research studies than standard computerised literature searches (Bareta et al., 1990; Larson et al., 1992b). In addition, review item reliability is high, usually achieving levels greater than 0.8 (Craigie et al., 1988; Larson et al., 1992b). Perhaps most importantly for reviews in controversial policy areas, SRs are replicable, and as such are ideal for issues where there may be greater potential for selection and interpretation biases (Levenson et al., 1990; Sackett, 1979).

While SRs have been used to assess the quality and quantity of research in specific areas (Larson et al., 1986; Larson et al., 1992; Larson et al., 1994), SR methodology has not yet been used to assess for selection and interpretation bias in published reviews. In order to test whether SR methodology could be used for such a purpose, the authors selected two reviews concerning an issue of policy controversy, post-abortion mental health status, which: 1) did not use specified review methodology; 2) covered a similar time frame; 3) cited peer-reviewed research; and 4) drew divergent conclusions. The authors applied the SR methodology to compare the two selected reviews and determine the presence and extent of selection and interpretation biases in this controversial area of policy concern.

METHOD

Review A, a 1991 *American Journal of Psychiatry* publication, reviewed the problems and strengths of the methods of research on the psychological sequelae of abortion, and provided summary interpretations of the findings (Dagg, 1991). Review B, published in 1989 in the *Psychiatric Journal of the University of Ottawa*, similarly assessed the quality of post-abortion research methodology and provided summary interpretations of the findings of the reviewed studies (Ney and Wickett, 1989).

Assessing selection bias
In order to assess selection bias, i.e. the degree to which the reviewers may have systematically erred in selecting the subjects (i.e., journal articles and research studies) for research review (Levenson et al., 1990; Sackett, 1979), each review's refereed journal citations concerning the emotional (i.e. psychiatric or psychological) sequelae of abortion were counted and compared. Book chapters and non-peer reviewed journal articles were excluded from the analyses according to past SR methods (Larson et al., 1986; Larson et al., 1992; Larson et al., 1994). Two studies cited in Review A were excluded from the evaluation because they were published in 1989 and 1990 respectively, and thus would not have been available for inclusion in Review B.

In addition to studies which focused specifically on the potential emotional or mental health effects of abortion, Review B included a section pertaining to potential physical effects of abortion. The latter section was excluded; only Review B references pertaining to the emotional sequelae of abortion were enumerated and compared to those found in Review A.

Assessing interpretation bias
After determining the number of peer-reviewed references concerning post-abortion emotional sequelae found in each review, the authors identified those references cited in common by each of the reviews. In order to assess interpretation bias—i.e., the degree to which each reviewer may have systematically erred in interpreting the study results, all common references were located. Each review's presentation of the content of the common

references was evaluated to determine whether the two reviews interpreted each reference's findings in a similar fashion. If a common reference was found to be represented differently by each review, each of the two review's explanations of the reference was included in Table I as an illustration of interpretation bias.

RESULTS

Selection bias
Review A included a total of 80 references concerning the emotional sequelae of abortion. Of these 80, 71 were published in peer-reviewed journals during the time frame which would have been accessible to Review B. Review B included a total of 108 references. Of these 108, 29 referred to physical health problems, while 53 were refereed journal articles concerning the emotional sequelae of abortion. Of the 71 relevant citations found in Review A and the 53 found in Review B, only 15 were found to be in common. Thus, only 21 per cent of Review A's citations and 28 per cent of Review B's citations were in common with the other review.

Interpretation bias
Of the 15 citations in common, 12 (80 per cent) offered similar interpretations, while 3 (20 per cent) presented dissimilar interpretations of the findings. The three common references and each reviewer's verbatim contrasting interpretations are documented in Table 1.

The first of the common references, the Freeman et al. study (1984) noted by Review A as one of the 'more objective studies', focused on the relative reduction in psychological distress before and after abortion, a finding seen as consistent with minimal emotional sequelae. Review B focused on the comparison of women seeking their first abortion with women seeking repeat abortions. According to Review B, women seeking repeat abortions (23 per cent of the sample) displayed evidence of equally distressed pre-abortion scores and more stressed post-abortion scores. Review B then used this data to support the conjecture that abortion does not always decrease psychological distress (as implied by Review A). Thus, while Freeman et al. may have presented both the instances in which abortion is associated with decreased psychological distress as well as the instances in which abortion is associated with increased psychological distress, both reviews chose to interpret the original study according to their own research review expectations.

Regarding the second study by Drower and Nash (1978), Review A reported findings that women denied abortions expressed greater guilt and anxiety than women who had abortions, implying a greater hazard from denied abortions than from performed abortions. Conversely, Review B reported that the study demonstrated nearly the opposite of that reported by Review A—that performed abortions were more emotionally hazardous than denied abortions. Review B reported findings that a follow-up of women who received abortions twelve to eighteen months after the abortion found that they were more likely to: 1) be in psychiatric treatment; 2) admit to a greater use of alcohol or tobacco 3) use more tranquilisers; and 4) experience more adverse personality changes and social isolation than those women who were denied abortions.

The third study by Jacobs et al. (1974) was reported by Review A as demonstrating the disappearance of psychopathological symptoms after an elective abortion. It should be noted that Review A cited the Jacobs et al. study as research evidence showing that the study subjects' pre-abortion MMPI scores on the Psychopathic Deviate, Schizophrenia, Hysteria, and Depression scales were higher than were their post-abortion scores—thus implying that abortion is associated with a decrease in emotional disturbance. In contrast, Review B cited the same study as an example of how abortion might be associated with increases in emotional disturbance for women with prior psychiatric problems. While it is very possible that Jacobs et al. might have found both a reduction in psychological problems for women after an abortion and an increase in psychological problems only for a single category of women, those who had a prior psychiatric history, what is surprising is the reporting of findings. The reviewers chose to report only those study results that supported their position.

DISCUSSION

Some effort at reliably assessing the body of post-abortion mental health research is both possible and necessary for improving the policy use of scientific research. In so doing, such research can limit ongoing national debate and policy uncertainty about such controversial issues. In comparing the results of these two reviews, the authors found significant differences in both the articles selected for review and the interpretation of the few articles common to both reviews. The fact that both of these reviews, published within eighteen months of each other shared only fifteen refereed journal references suggests the strong potential for selection bias by both reviews. If reviews are, in theory, conducted to examine objectively all of the published research on a particular subject, such as mental health status following an abortion, in order to arrive at a consensus on an issue, it would appear that both of these reviews have fallen short of that goal. Indeed, each review seems to have more subjectively rather than objectively surveyed the literature and selected individual studies which supported their review conjecture, while choosing to exclude literature that may have presented contradictory results.

Even when both reviews included common studies, another methodological deficiency was documented—interpretation bias. Of the fifteen common studies shared by both Review A and Review B, one-fifth were interpreted with nearly opposite findings. While both reviews may not have purposefully distorted the findings of the common studies, each review author seems to have interpreted articles to fit the slant of their own review. Thus, even when selection bias is overcome and both reviews include the same study, in 20 per cent of cases the reviews suffer from interpretation bias with reviewers interpreting articles to fit the theme of their review.

On the basis of these findings the authors suggest that future reviews, particularly in controversial social policy research areas such as post abortion mental health which receive constant media as well as legislative attention, would benefit from the use of SR methodology in order to provide a more objective and replicable identification of the studies for the review, as well as a more reliable classification of the review results. Both methodological steps—identification of articles and interpretation of the content—are necessary in order to minimise discrepancies between review of the same subject.

When research reviews have the potential for significant public policy implications, such as those conducted on the subject of abortion, it should be possible for other investigators to replicate the results of a review, regardless of their own position on a topic. But when personal bias and non-research agendas enter into the review process, as the findings of this study imply, the authority and credibility of the research process is undermined.

Reviews of research do not achieve their intended goal when they are in actuality either a commentary or editorial use of research to support the reviewer's personal views. The authors believe that it is time for policy research reviews to begin to hold to the same standards of sample selection, reliability, and validity that are held for original clinical research. While opinions can play a role in research, commentaries and editorials are usually intended for this purpose; research reviews are not. For research reviews to fail to approach a review of a field of inquiry in a reliable and replicable manner invites research misuse, if not abuse. More specifically, such methodological deficiencies invite published commentaries masquerading as reviews.

REFERENCES

Bareta, J.C., Larson, D.B., Lyons, J.S., and Zorc, J.J.: 'A comparison of manual and MEDLARS reviews of the literature on consultation-liaison psychiatry'. *American Journal of Psychiatry*, 1990, 147:1040-2.

Craigie, F.C.; Liu, I.Y.; Larson, D.B.; and Lyons, J.S.: 'A systematic analysis of religious variables in the *Journal of Family Practice*, 1976-1986'. *Journal of Family Practice*, 1988, 27:509-13.

Dagg, P.K.: 'The psychological sequelae of therapeutic abortion—denied and completed'. *American Journal of Psychiatry*, 1991, 148:578-85.

Drower, S.A.; and Nash, E.S.: 'Therapeutic abortion on psychiatric grounds'. *South African Medical Journal*, 1978, 54:604-8.

Freeman, E.W.; Rickels, K.; Huggins, G.R.; Garcia, C.; and Polin, J.: 'Emotional distress patterns among women having first and repeat abortions'. *Obstetrics and Gynecology*, 1984, 55:630-6.

Jacobs, D.; Garcia, C.R.; Rickels, K.; and Prencel, R.W.: 'A prospective study on the psychological effects of therapeutic abortion'. *Comprehensive Psychiatry*, 1974, 15:422-34.

Larson, D.B.; Pattison, E.M.; Blazer, D.G.; Omran, A.R.; and Kaplan, B.H.: 'Systematic analysis of research on religious variables in four major psychiatric journals, 1978-1982'. *American Journal of Psychiatry*, 1986, 143:329-34.

Larson, D.B.; Lyons, J.S.; Hohmann, A.A.; et al.: 'A systematic review of nursing home research in three psychiatric journals: 1966-1985'. *International Journal of Geriatric Psychiatry*, 1988, 4:129-34.

Larson, D.B.; Pastro, L.E.; Lyons, J.S.; and Anthony, E.: 'The systematic review: An innovative approach to reviewing research'. Department of Health and Human Services, Washington, D.C., 1992a.

Larson, D.B.; Sherrill, K.A.; Lyons, J.S.; et al.: 'Associations between dimensions of religious commitment and mental health reported in *American Journal of Psychiatry* and *Archives of General Psychiatry*: 1978-1989'. *American Journal of Psychiatry*, 1992b, 149:557-9.

Larson, D.B.; Sheriill, K.A.; and Lyons, J.S.: 'Neglect and misuse of the "R word": Systematic reviews of religious measures in health, mental health, and aging'. In *Religion, Aging, and Health: Theoretical Foundations and Methodological Frontiers*. Edited by Levin, JS. Sage Publications, Newbury Park: CA, 1994.

Levenson, J.L.; Colenda, C.; Larson, D.B.; and Bareta, J.C.: 'Methodology in consultation-liaison research: A clarification of biases'. *Psychosomatics*, 1990, 31:367-76.

Mulrow, C.D.: 'The medical review article: State of the science'. *Annals of Internal Medicine*, 1987, 106:485-88.

Ney, P.G., and Wickett, A.R.: 'Mental health and abortion: Review and analysis'. *Psychiatric Journal of the University of Ottawa*, 1989, 14:506-14.

Sackett, D.L.: 'Bias in analytic research'. *Journal of Chronic Disease*, 1979, 32:51-61.

Sherrill, K.A.; Larson, D.B.; and Greenwold, M.A.: 'Is religion taboo in gerontology? Systematic review of research on religion in three major gerontology journals, 1985-1991'. *American Journal of Geriatric Psychiatry*, 1993, 1:109-17.

Table 1

Central Findings in Quote Form, Review A

Freeman et al.: *Decrease of SCL-90 scores after abortion*—'Freeman et al, in one of the more objective studies involving over 400 women, found that SCL-90 scores were elevated on several subscales in women before the procedure but decreased significantly toward normal quite rapidly after the abortion. Those scales on which the pre-abortion scores were highest, indicating the highest level of distress, had the greatest decrease after the abortion.'

Central Findings in Quote Form, Review B

Foreman et al.: *Repeat aborters have no decrease in stress levels* —'. . . comparing first and repeat induced abortions state, "Elevated stress levels were similar in both groups prior to the abortion procedures, particularly depression, anxiety and somatisation." "After abortion, repeat aborters continued to have significantly higher emotional distress scores in dimensions relating to interpersonal relationships." This American study, reported in 1980, found 35 per cent were repeat aborters compared to a 23 per cent repeat rate reported in 1976. The finding that pre-abortion scores of repeaters were the same as those of first aborters suggested that familiarity with the experience "(of abortion) did not decrease emotional distress. Repeat abortion patients remained significantly higher on scores of interpersonal sensitivity, paranoid ideation, chronic anxiety, and sleep disturbance. Women repeating abortions had higher scores on dimensions of somatisation, hostility, and psychoticism. The pre- and post- abortion emotional distress scores and demographic attributes of their sample were similar to those of a sample of abortion patients in the same hospital in 1973." "The similarity of findings suggest that ready access to abortion services in the intervening five years since the Supreme Court decision, did not alone diminish the stress associated with abortion".'

Drower and Nash: *Denied abortion more harmful than abortion*—'... those women denied abortion expressed greater guilt and anxiety than women for whom an abortion had been performed.'

Drower and Nash: *Abortion more harmful than denied abortion*—'One study that comes close to randomising abortion in two very similar groups of women, found that abortion is more hazardous than refused abortion. This study by S. Drower and E. Nash found no significant difference when comparing variables in their sample between those women whose pregnancy was aborted and those refused an abortion, i.e., those with disrupted family background, illegitimate, adopted or fostered, school difficulties, poor socialisation, previous psychiatric treatment, previous suicide attempts, poor self-image, and only an equivocal difference in the number referred for psychiatric treatment. Twelve to eighteen months after the initial presentation, a greater proportion who were terminated were under psychiatric treatment, admitted to a greater increase in the use of alcohol or tobacco, used more tranquilisers, experienced more adverse personality changes and had more social isolation than those who were not terminated.'

Jacobs et al.: *Disappearance of psychopathological symptoms after abortion*—'A study by Jacobs et al., who used women undergoing minor gynecologic surgery as control subjects showed higher pre-abortion scores for the pregnant women on the Psychopathic Deviate, Schizophrenia, Hysteria, and Depression scales of the MMPI; these differences disappeared after the abortion.'

Jacobs et al.: *More adverse emotional sequelae after abortion for women with past psychiatric history*—'In reports where the psychiatric status of patients before abortion is stated, the evidence clearly indicates that adverse emotional sequelae are more common and more serious when there is a history of psychiatric ill health.'

Post-abortion syndrome ...
Is it a reality? Methodological issues

C.V.R. BLACKER

In the United Kingdom one fifth of all pregnancies currently end in induced termination whilst rates are as high as one third in inner city areas.

When considering the possible sequelae to abortion one must recognise that there are several spheres of life in which these might be made manifest ... emotional, psychological, social (including relationships) and spiritual. The problems of *quantifying* these are immense and many are subject to interpretation which can lead different people to completely opposite conclusions. For example, our review of the published literature on termination of pregnancy over the last two decades (Zolese & Blacker, 1992) concluded that approximately 10 per cent of women experience ongoing adverse psychological sequelae in the medium term (i.e. up to one year). We have since been congratulated on this article by pro-abortionists who see it as demonstrating that abortion is a relatively benign event and also by *anti*-abortionists who see it as confirming *their* view that abortion is *not* an innocent event from the psychological point of view. In fact, much of our article was taken up with showing that the older studies of the psychological outcome of abortion were flawed because of a lack of reliable and standardised criteria for measuring many of the important facets of post-abortion syndrome such as guilt or depression. The development of *new* standardised psychiatric instruments and rating scales has gone some way towards clarifying the situation and permitted a more reliable analysis of the rates of formal *psychiatric disorder* than the somewhat impressionistic data obtained from earlier studies. Nonetheless, extensive areas remain undefined and unstandardised and essentially unmeasurable using existing instruments. The problem is particularly acute in the case of *spiritual* sequelae such as loss or diminution of faith, unresolved spiritual guilt, reduction in religious activity (such as prayer) or altered views of the character and nature of God.

Much of the evidence about a post-abortion syndrome seems to be accumulating in letters to magazines and newspapers, through individual case histories of women presenting to counsellors and psychiatrists, through the confessional and through those who present to deliverance ministry teams. Although undoubtedly important from the point of view of the sufferer, from the epidemiological (and therefore scientific) point of view they have a relatively low impact. One feature of these anecdotal accounts is that the declaration seems to occur many years after the index event . . . in some cases ten or twenty years later or, in the case of the confessional, perhaps even on a person's deathbed. If this time scale is an accurate one, then there would be very considerable practical difficulties in conducting a suitable prospective outcome study acceptable, from the methodological point of view, to the scientific establishment. Moreover, the late reporting of many of these experiences raises the question whether intercurrent events, the passage of time, the process of internal reflection, spiritual development, general maturation or other subsequent experiences such as abortion by one's daughter might have been instrumental not only in shaping but in some cases *creating* for the first time the guilt which is expressed as a key feature of post-abortion syndrome? One elegant example of this is the study of psychiatric disorder in pregnancy by Kumar & Robson (1984). These authors found that a history of a previous termination was a risk factor for the emergence of new psychological difficulties and distress in the first trimester of a subsequent and *wanted* pregnancy. In many cases the psychological difficulty arising from the termination had remained dormant (and possibly justified) untll awoken by the subsequent pregnancy and thoughts of motherhood. There is an undoubted strong social pressure to deny psychological emotional or spiritual difficulties after an event such as termination of pregnancy. There is often an additional conspiracy of silence surrounding the event which is known only to the patient's mother and not always revealed to the baby's father. Sometimes even the woman's general practitioner doesn't know about the abortion and there is a strong disincentive to talk about the abortion and any feelings of regret to others. Such denial is likely to be maximal soon after the abortion has taken place and at a time when most women are in contact with services which are able to offer counselling. The existence of denial is also likely to artificially *reduce* the reported prevalence of psychological distress in *short-term* outcome studies. It took many years for physical and sexual abuse of children to come to light and to be recognised for the phenomenon it was; indeed, Freud made his reputation on his assumption that those patients who reported such abuses to him must have been fantasising!

It is likely that this attitude of denial (as occurs so often in the case of other traumatic or 'shameful' experiences such as bereavement or rape) may serve to perpetuate or even inflame the associated psychological suffering.

This introduces us to a further difficulty which is that patients who, for various reasons (including religious), have difficulty accepting a termination, might be those very women who do worse in the long term. Women without scruples might therefore be expected to adjust more quickly to termination. Likewise, women undergoing termination in countries in which it is generally disapproved of or in particularly religious societies might be expected to have a *higher* incidence of post-abortion syndrome than those in so-called liberal or 'enlightened' societies. This is in fact the case: studies of the psychiatric sequelae show that coming from a religious background or having a personal religious orientation is one of the risk factors for subsequent psychological difficulty. As shown in our review there are other risk factors which fall into the religious domain and which might pose a significant challenge *vis-à-vis* the *interpretation of findings*:

> women who are ambivalent towards terminating their pregnancy
> women how have a poor relationship with their own mother
> women who are in sexual relationships that are unstable
> women with more severe psychological disturbances at the time they *present* for abortion, and
> older women who have several children already living.

In such cases the pro-abortionists might well argue that it is not the *termination per se* which is responsible for the distress a woman experiences but the unrealistic expectations of those around her and the religion in which she has been raised. This takes us back to my first point which is that there is an important difference between the clinical observations themselves and the *interpretation* one subsequently *places* on those observations which one needs to clarify before conducting research on something as value-laden as post-abortion syndrome.

Of course, having a heightened moral sensitivity (such as in religious people) doesn't necessarily mean that religious belief is itself harmful; the opposite interpretation is equally valid, i.e. that it is those whose moral consciences have been seared by years of sin and self-indulgence who have now lost the capacity to experience concern, regret or revulsion over the termination of a life. Indeed, it may well be that a loss of moral sensitivity may be one of the specifically *spiritual* features of a post-abortion syndrome. One could test this by examining moral attitudes amongst women who have had one two or more terminations, although it would be necessary to control for a whole host of other variables as well before one could speak conclusively on this point. Nonetheless, this loss of moral sensitivity or spiritual decay and death is an important Biblical principle as shown by Paul's epistle to the Romans. In fact, when seen from a Christian Biblical perspective the whole post-abortion syndrome could be turned on its head, i.e. the patient who *does* experience distress and guilt after an abortion is in fact showing an appropriate response and it is the woman who *fails* to do so whose spiritual or moral health is suspect. If this hypothesis were correct then, from God's perspective, the more malignant post-abortion syndrome would be the one in which there is no apparent concern or distress . . . just the steady dying of the spirit within. This remark is not intended as a personal judgement; I have to work everyday with women who have had abortions and it is not my place to judge or criticise them. However, as a Christian psychiatrist I find it helpful to recognise that God's law and threatened judgments in this life are manifestations of His grace and designed principally to lead men and women to repentance. God threatens (and sometimes chastises) because he wants to 'come to our senses and so be saved' (2 Tim 2:26). As a clinician this enables me to place a *positive* and *therapeutic* interpretation on any guilt or depression a patient discloses to me as a result of behaviour in the past. If this view is correct, then perhaps researchers should stop concentrating on the *well* (i.e. those who feel guilty) and start looking at what happens to the unwell (those who don't). . . .

One factor which continues to dog outcome research into post-abortion syndrome is the difficulty in obtaining follow-up. Many women simply aren't available or don't wish to be available for re-interview. Partly this is a phenomenon of denial, partly one of guilt and partly because some women who get pregnant and then request an abortion are living chaotic and irresponsible lifestyles. The phenomenon of the abortion-recidivist would be worth studying in this respect. What is it about these women that leads them to repeatedly use abortion as a form of contraception? What is their moral and spiritual status? What happens to their relationships? Do they ever settle down? Are they blessed and prospering or do they go on to experience further adversity? Do they ever truly know peace or do they become, as St Paul said, degraded and spiritually dead? Important questions these.

With these thoughts in mind a successful and rigorous study of the post-abortion syndrome would therefore need to try and control for factors such as religious orientation not only in the woman but also in members of her family, her degree of ambivalence at the time of presentation, the stability of the existing relationship and the interactive effect of previous terminations and existing children. One would also need to control for other factors including the *procedure* of abortion . . . where it takes place and how, who conducts it and the attitude of the staff around them. For example, in some centres women presenting for abortion are admitted to gynaecological wards alongside women being investigated for infertility. Pre-abortion counselling is not always available and, if so, the woman's partner doesn't always accompany her. All these factors are important in determining *what* subsequent reaction, if any, there will be to a termination. There are so many other factors going on, such as threat of a breakup of the existing relationship because of the pregnancy, parental disapproval, loss of employment etc. which make it hard (if not impossible) to pinpoint *which* adverse psychological sequelae could be attributed to the abortion and which to other factors.

Some of these risk factors associated with poor psychological adjustment to a termination of pregnancy may also contribute to the woman becoming pregnant in the first place; many of those requesting abortion are suffering from fairly longstanding social and relationship difficulties which make independent contributions to psychological ill health. Pregnancy itself also carries a small risk of psychiatric disorder which is difficult to disentangle from the psychological effects of abortion. Not all women react positively to finding that they are pregnant even if they subsequently decide to keep the baby. Many young girls deliberately get pregnant to get out of the family home (some to escape sexual abuse) or to obtain a council flat for which they would otherwise wait several years.

Thus, when we talk about the psychological sequelae of abortion we are in fact looking at an immensely complicated field rendered all the more complex by the passage of time and subsequent reinterpretation of events. There is also the phenomenon of an *interaction* between these various factors . . . the circumstances of the pregnancy, the pregnancy itself, the mother's background, personality and social circumstances, the attitude of those around her etc. . . . all of which need to be taken into account and analysed using special statistical techniques. For example, one such risk factor may not in itself have much effect; however, the presence of *two* factors may have an independent effect upon a third (e.g. the primary sexual relationship or the woman's own self-esteem) which then determines whether that will respond *differently* to a fourth and/or subsequent events (e.g. whether she accepts counselling, or confesses to a priest, or takes drugs or gets pregnant again).

Very little is known about what factors might exist which *protect* against the development of psychological problems; one acknowledges the possible beneficial effects of counselling, although this is not always available especially in the private clinics. Studies tend to concentrate on the *negative* impact of different psychosocial variables; studies which sought to determine what *protective* or ameliorating variables might exist need to be designed (and analysed) in a different way. Of course, to discover whether there are protective factors one needs to *examine* for them in the first place; otherwise the data won't be available for analysis. Personality attributes are likely to be one important source of protection, e.g. general resilience in the face of adversity or the good self-esteem which springs from having had a secure and happy childhood.

In the face of all these difficulties the best way to proceed in the study of the post-abortion syndrome is to do so slowly, not trying to be too ambitious, and building slowly on the foundations laid by previous workers. It would also be helpful if someone were able to conduct an in-depth descriptive study of these women who write to magazines reporting their experience of post-abortion guilt to see whether there are any recurring themes which could be incorporated in subsequent studies and to see whether they differ in any way from other, carefully-matched, women who have not had terminations or from those who have but who haven't developed these symptom. Finally, we should perhaps be looking in a completely different direction; instead of expecting to see damage in the area of those who do experience guilt, we should be concentrating more on those who *don't* and seeing what happens to *them*.

What is the effect of previous terminations on a woman's attitude towards subsequent children? Are societies which encourage a liberal attitude towards abortion distinguished by their caring attitude towards children in general, or are children seen as commodities that can be dealt with on a sale-or-return basis? There is already a wealth of data showing that unwanted children are at risk of developing delinquency and other behavioural disturbances, and perhaps we in the West are now reaping the harvest of a devalued regard for life which has been ushered in on the tide of abortion (and now euthanasia).

Rates for euthanasia and suicide vary greatly from culture to culture and it is clear that the prevailing attitudes within a society determine whether someone *will* actually take their life or request an abortion. Now that abortion is an accepted practice in the UK it is likely that *fewer* women are upset by it than they were in the past. Although this fact will be hailed by many as a *good* thing it does not necessarily indicate that society is in a state of *good* moral health; a society which becomes inured to certain evils presents an ideal culture medium for further evils to germinate and develop. Without exaggeration, euthanasia (for which abortion has paved the way) is probably the greatest moral threat our society has had to face for a very long time. In the case of euthanasia it is not the arguments for and against it in this or that particular *case* which constitute the threat, but the *wider* implications such decisions have for the *rest* of society once and if euthanasia becomes widely available. Abortion is another case in point. Therefore, simultaneous to any further research on the post-abortion syndrome in individual cases, we also need to examine the wider issues and the impact on society as a whole in sociological studies which, in the long run, are of equal importance.

REFERENCES

R. Kumar amd K. Robson (1984), 'A prospective study of emotional disorders in childbearing women', *British Journal of Psychiatry*, 144, 35-47.

G. Zolese and C.V.R. Blacker (1992), 'Psychological sequelae of therapeutic abortion . . . a review', *British Journal of Psychiatry*, 160, 742-9.

Abortion: psychological indications and consequences

AGNETA SUTTON

ABORTION—AN INSTITUTIONAL PRACTICE

In 1938 the first steps were taken to liberalise abortion law so as to allow abortion not merely to preserve the life of the mother but also to prevent her physical or mental breakdown. Subsequently, the criteria for abortion were to become gradually vaguer, mainly because mental criteria could be interpreted differently. Eventually, with the Abortion Act 1967, the indications for abortion were expanded, beyond both the preservation of the woman's life and the preservation of her physical and mental health, to include the preservation of the physical and mental health of any existing children of her family in addition to the eugenic criteria. The one restriction that remained was that the abortion had to be performed before the 28th week of pregnancy or before the child was viable outside the maternal body; except if the abortion were performed to save the mother's life. With the amendment to the 1967 Act incorporated in the Human Fertilisation and Embryology Act 1990, even this restriction was removed. Today, abortion up to the time of birth is permitted: to prevent permanent injury to the woman's physical or mental health; or, if the continuation of the pregnancy entails a greater risk to the woman's life than its interruption; or, if there is a substantial risk that the child would be born seriously handicapped. A limit of 24 weeks gestation is imposed for abortion on less serious grounds; namely, when the pregnancy would involve some, but not permanent, injury to the mother's physical or mental health or when the continuation of the pregnancy would constitute a great danger, not to the life but to the physical or mental well-being of the mother, than its termination.

Within the introduction of liberal abortion legislation such as the English—or that in the United States, which allows abortion on demand during the first trimester—abortion has become an institutionalised, publicly sanctioned and frequently performed practice. The abortion rate in England is about one in five pregnancies; much the same ratio as in the United States.

However, the fact that abortion is the responsibility of a profession acting in accordance with state regulations and is generally regarded as medical treatment, raises a number of very important moral and philosophical questions. Can one rightly regard abortion as medical *treatment*? Is it in accord with the Hippocratic tradition of medicine? Or, with the Judeo-Christian principle of respect for the sanctity of human life? To what extent, if any, is abortion ever of therapeutic value? Finally, what effect will it have on society?

This paper examines the reasons why women have abortions and the psychological effects abortions may have on them. It is argued that many past studies concerning the indications for abortion and its consequence have suffered from methodological shortcomings and that insufficient attention has been paid to the long-term effects of abortion, to suppression and to delayed reactions. These findings have important implications for the answers to the questions posed above.

WHY DO WOMEN HAVE ABORTIONS?

Despite the advance of medicine, a small number of abortions are still undertaken with a view to preserving the woman's physical health. A certain number of abortions are undertaken for eugenic reasons. But by far the greatest proportion of abortions are undertaken for social reasons. Regarding psychiatric indications, these would seem to range from conditions that are clinically diagnosable, such as stress and anxiety in connection with various adverse social conditions.

Many recent studies show that a large amount of previously reported research on the psychiatric indications for abortion are unreliable inasmuch as they tend to exaggerate the adverse psychological consequences of pregnancy. The explanation for this may be that, before the abortion laws were liberalised to include social indications and future expected psychological consequences of giving birth to a child, a woman seeking an abortion on psychiatric grounds would have had to show actual psychiatric disturbance in order that the abortion be legally acceptable (Gibbons, 1984).

But if most abortions are performced for social or stress-related social reasons, what are the main social reasons in question? Some information may be gained from statistics reported in *Family Planning Perspective* in 1988, indicating that three-quarters of the women interviewed desired an abortion because having a child would interfere with work, school or other social responsibilities, that about two-thirds wanted an abortion for financial reasons, and that one half did not want to be a single parent or had relationship problems with the father (Torres and Forrest, 1988).

Unmarried or divorced women seem to resort to abortion more frequently than married women. Indeed, according to the statistics of the Society for the Protection of Unborn Children (SPUC), abortions carried out on single women in Great Britain between 1969 and 1989 increased, not only in absolute numbers but also as a proportion of all abortions—and now account for two-thirds of the total (SPUC, 1992). According to another study published in *Family Planning Perspective* in 1990, 'in most Western European and English-speaking countries, about half of the abortions are obtained by young, unmarried women seeking to delay a first birth, while in Eastern Europe and the developing countries, abortion is most common among married women with two or more children' (Henshaw, 1990).

On the assumption that a single mother's worries are mostly of a financial kind and related to the problem of combining education or work to earn money with child-care and good mothering, one must surely question the prescribed remedy—especially if it is widely prescribed. Of course, a number of women would choose an abortion even if they were offered other alternatives. Nevertheless, would it not be more appropriate and show a more caring attitude on the part of society to improve the conditions of single mothers rather than to offer them an abortion? It might be financially cheaper for society (at least in the short-term) to offer single women abortions than to offer them realistic social benefits together with housing and good nursery places, but there may be a high moral price to pay for such a policy. This will be the case if many women suffer adverse psychological consequences or if their families do so.

SOME WOMEN ARE AT SPECIAL RISK OF ADVERSE PSYCHOLOGICAL CONSEQUENCES

Psychiatric conditions have been regarded as one of the main indications for abortion. But a number of recent studies show that abortion is not a suitable remedy for such conditions. On the contrary, it would appear that abortion is contra-indicated when psychiatric disease is present (Ney and Wickett, 1989; Gibbons 1984; Rosenfeldt, 1992). A report by two British doctors is especially convincing (Zolese and Blacker, 1992).This report is based on a survey of a vast number of studies undertaken since the 1960s. On the whole, the authors view abortion favourably and claim that most of the examined studies showed that abortion *per se* does not cause psychiatric disturbance. Nevertheless, they point out that certain categories of women are at special risk of negative consequences, among them women with a previous psychiatric history or with psychological disturbances at the time of presentation. Other studies have shown that post-partum psychoses carry a good prognosis, post-abortion psychoses carry a relatively poor one (Sim and Neisser, 1979; David, Rasmussen and Holst, 1981).

Not only are women with a history of psychiatric problems at special risk of adverse psychological reactions after an abortion, but so too are certain other categories of women. A number of studies indicate that women who have an ambivalent attitude towards abortion, who feel they have been coerced and who abort for health reasons are at special risk (Gibbons, 1984). Some researchers add the following risk factors: religious objections to abortion; lack of support from spouses, partners, parents or others and abortions on ground of foetal abnormality. Older multiparous women may also be at risk (Zolese and Blacker, 1992; Barnett, Freudenberg and Wille, 1986).

Maternal—and also paternal—grief and trauma are often particularly acute after an abortion for eugenic reasons. This is hardly surprising. When abortions are performed on fetal indications, there is usually no other reason why the mother should feel that she needs an abortion. In addition, the parents or mothers often harbour feelings of guilt and feel it is their fault the child is not alright. To give an example, it was found in a British study involving 48 women, who had had eugenic abortions, that 37 of them (77 per cent) experienced an acute grief reaction immediately and that 22 (46 per cent) remained symptomatic six months after the termination of the pregnancy, some of them requiring psychiatric support (Lloyd and Laurence, 1985).

Teenage abortions also seem especially problematic and some studies report very disturbing findings. One study described in *Adolescence* in 1988, examined the differences between 35 women who had had abortions in their teens and 36 women who had had abortions after the age of 20. The psychiatric histories of the women before the abortion were reported, as were the psychological consequences of the abortion. Antisocial and paranoid personality disorders, as well as drug abuse and psychotic delusions, were found to be significantly higher among those who had had abortions in their teens. It was argued that the trauma of abortion during these sensitive and formative years could cause significant disruption of personality development (Campbell, Franco and Jurs, 1988).

WHAT PERCENTAGE OF WOMEN ARE AFFECTED—AND HOW AFFECTED ARE THEY?

It may be difficult to quantify exactly the proportion of women who suffer psychological complications after an abortion and even more difficult to say exactly how deeply affected these women are. Yet, it is clear that many studies are inadequate inasmuch as they take account only of short-term or relatively short-term effects. In order to have a fuller picture of the consequences of abortion it is clearly necessary to follow the women—and their families—over many years.

Nevertheless, before considering the need for long-term studies, let us examine the findings of a few short-term studies comparing the women's mental state before the abortion with their mental state immediately or shortly afterwards. In a study of self-reported reactions, which involved 158 women, 45 per cent reported satisfaction several months after the abortion and over half reported an improved outlook on life. The authors evidently regarded these findings as positive. Yet they are hardly impressive, especially as the authors themselves indicated that about 10 per cent of the women would benefit from counselling, because they reported guilt-feelings and confusion (Burnell and Norflect, 1987). A German study involving 117 women interviewed before the abortion and a year later reported that one year after the abortion about 14 per cent were still in a state of emotional imbalance and that 7 per cent were clearly impaired emotionally and in their everyday functioning. Depression before the abortion was correlated with an increased risk of depression after the abortion. Thus 21 per cent of the women who had problems after the abortion had been more depressed than the others before the abortion (Barnett, Freudenberg and Wille, 1986). Finally, in a British study involving 64 women, it was found that about 44 per cent of the women interviewed a couple of months after their abortion had trouble with their nerves, 36 per cent had sleep disturbance and 5 per cent had received prescriptions for psychotropic drugs (Ashton, 1980).

SHORT-TERM EFFECTS MUST BE DISTINGUISHED FROM LONG-TERM AND DELAYED EFFECTS

The medical profession, perhaps psychoanalysts and psychiatrists in particular, are becoming increasingly aware of delayed reactions and long-term effects of abortions. It is not surprising if a women feels relief initially after an abortion. The operation is over; the pregnancy with all its problems is over; she is still alive. But this does not mean that she will not have trouble later. As the US Surgeon General Everett Koop said when testifying in the US House of Representatives in 1989, after having studied over 250 articles pertaining to the risk of abortion, 'short-term studies could be highly misleading'. Women react to abortion in very different ways. Some women, who do not show any negative symptoms during the first few months after the abortion, do so years later. Other women may suffer very little or no visible damage at any stage, while some will suffer both immediate and permanent damage.

Anne Speckhard and Vincent Rue, two eminent American authorities, argue that psychological complications after abortions may be divided into three kinds: post-abortion distress, post-abortion psychosis and post-abortion syndrome (Speckhard and Rue, 1992).

According to this scheme, reactions are classified as post-abortion distress if they occur within three months of the abortion and persist for no more than six months. Among the symptoms are physical pain, emotional stress, a sense of loss, personality conflict and relationship problems with husbands or partners and disorientation in the person's sense of values.

Post-abortion psychosis is a general term for major affective or thought disorders not present before, but directly attributable to, the abortion. It is said to be characterised by chronic and severe symptoms of disorganisation and significant personality and reality problems, such as hallucinations, delusions, paranoia and severe depression. The authors say this condition is rare.

Post-abortion syndrome is understood as a type of 'post-traumatic stress disorder'. The criteria for post traumatic stress disorder have been specified in the *American Psychiatric Association, Diagnostic and Statistical Manual of Mental Disorders*, 1987 (p. 250), as a state caused by 'an event that is outside the range of usual human experience . . . e.g., . . . serious threat to one's life or physical integrity, serious threat or harm to one's children . . . or seeing another person who has been or is being seriously injured or killed as the result of . . . physical violence' (Rue, 1978). British soldiers who have witnessed atrocities in Bosnia are being counselled to overcome this kind of stress disorder. Many Vietnam soldiers also suffered from this condition. Typical features are memory flashbacks or re-experiencing of the violent event, nightmares, anniversary reactions, reduced responsiveness to others and delayed reactions to the experience. For the condition to be defined as post-abortion traumatic stress disorder, the symptoms of re-experience and associated reactions must persist for more than one month. The onset of the symptoms may be delayed by six months or more after the event. Furthermore, according to the findings reported by Speckhard and Rue, the patients do not normally recover spontaneously (Speckhard and Rue, 1992).

ABORTION — A SOCIALLY UNRECOGNISED LOSS

It is noteworthy that the post-abortion syndrome may be difficult to identify. One reason is that abortion is a socially unrecognised loss. The woman is supposed to experience relief—not grief. The existence and death of her unborn child is not recognised by others around her. Yet, her body would have told her that she was with child and she may, even if unconsciously, have begun bonding with the child. To help the woman to cope, all sorts of defence mechanisms might be at work. Some women, so it would appear, manage to suppress or forget their abortion altogether; others merely for a long time. Janet Mattinson of the Institute of Marital Studies in London, emphasises the need to take into account delayed grief reactions (Mattinson, 1985). As clues to suppressed emotional responses, she points to anniversary reactions, which may take the form of headaches, abdominal or chest pains, or gynaecological symptoms, which occur around the anniversary date of the abortion or the date the baby was due to be born. Others have made similar observations, and it has been found that often the patients themselves do not associate such symptoms with their abortion (Franco, Campbell, Tamburrin, Jurs, Penz, Evans, 1989). The onset of delayed symptoms tends to be triggered by the birth or loss of another child or some other event associated with children or reproduction, such as subsequent infertility or menopause (Speckhard and Rue, 1992).

FATHERS AND SIBLINGS

Another point of note is that abortions affect not only the women themselves but also their spouses or partners. Thus it would appear that some fathers of aborted babies need as much—or more—attention as their wives or girl-friends. Also, marital and relationship problems are not infrequent after an abortion experience (Mattinson, 1985). It has been noted that there is a tendency for non-marital relationships to break up after an abortion (Gardner, 1972).

Children whose mothers have aborted might also be affected. Phillip Ney has carried out extensive research regarding the subject of child abuse. In one of his earlier articles on this issue, he shows that 'death of Canadian children from social causes rapidly increased after early abortion became available on demand in Canada in 1969 and that British Columbia and Ontario with the highest rates of abortion are also the provinces with the highest rates of child abuse'. He also shows that there is a statistical correlation between child abuse and abortion in the United States and that, since 1972 when first-trimester abortion became available on demand, there has been a significant increase in child battering (Ney, 1979).

It is possible that the correlation between the rates of abortion and child abuse is a mere coincidence. And, of course an abortion experience could have the opposite effect and make a woman over-protective of a subsequent child. Nevertheless, according to Ney, having an abortion might decrease a woman's instinctual restraint against violence towards her young. One explanation for this, he says, is that the women's ability to bond with subsequent children might be impaired by the experience. In his view, first pregnancy abortion might be especially vulnerable in this respect.

In another article Ney and a co-author describe what they call the 'survivor syndrome' and point out that children are becoming increasingly aware that they have been chosen. While they admit that there has been little research in this area, the authors warn that there may be hazards to a child's development, if it realises that a sibling has been aborted (Ney and Wickett, 1989).

CONCLUSION

There is, it would seem, increasing evidence that adverse post-abortion reactions are a widespread phenomenon (not confined to women), that in many cases the reactions only surface years after the event and that often they are not recognised or diagnosed for what they are. In the light of this evidence, it is surely time for health authorities and medical establishments to undertake coordinated, international, large-scale studies of the social and psychological consequences of abortion—and, indeed, to review the whole practice of abortion.

Of course, for those of us who view foetal life as individual human life, there can be no doubt that abortion is contrary both to the principle of the sanctity of human life and to the Hippocratic norm of medicine never to harm. However, we live in a pluralist society and not everyone takes this view of foetal life. But even those who defend the woman's right to choose ought to ask themselves whether a more restrictive policy might not do less harm to women and to society in the long run. It should be noted that abortion may affect women not only psychologically but also physically, sometimes causing serious damage to their health and reproductive ability.

In short, those who are pro-choice can no longer avoid facing the question whether the medical profession has not betrayed its own principle to do no harm in allowing itself to become a legally sanctioned instrument of abortion, and on a massive scale. Indeed, it would seem that the practice of abortion is one of the major societal self-delusions of our time.

ACKNOWLEDGEMENTS

I wish to express my special gratitude to Dr Michael Jarmulowicz, who kindly allowed me to study the extensive research material he has collected on the physical and psychological effects of abortion. I also wish to thank SPUC and British Victims of Abortion for letting me share their statistics and many of their studies. Finally, I am indebted to Dr Peter Doherty for lending his material on the aftermath of abortion.

REFERENCES

Ashton, J.R., 'Psychological Outcome of Induced Abortion', *British Journal of Obstetrics and Gynaecology*, 1980, 87, 115-22.

Barnett, W., Freudenberg, N. and Wille, R., 'Regional Prospective Study of Psychiatric Sequelae of Legal Abortion', *Fortschritte Neurologia Psychiatria*, 1986, 54 (4), 106-18.

Burnell, G.M. and Norfleet, M.A., 'Women's Self-reported responses to Abortion', *British Journal of Psychology*, 1987, 121 (1), 7176.

Campbell, N.B.; Franco, K.; and Jurs, S., 'Abortion in Adolescence', *Adolescence*, 1988, 23 (92), 813-23.

David, Henry P.; Rasmussen, Niels, K.; and Holst Erik, 'Postpartum and Postabortion Psychotic Reactions', *Family Planning Perspectives*, 1981, 13 (2), 92.

Franco, K.; Campbell, K.; Tamburrino M.; Jurs, S.; Penz J. and Evans C., 'Anniversary Reactions and Due Date Responses following Abortion', *Psychotherapy and Psychosomatics*, 1989, 52, 151-4.

Gardner, R.F., *Abortion: The Personal Dilemmaa*, Exeter, 1972, 209-21.

Gibbons, Mary, 'Psychiatric Sequelae of Induced Abortion', *Journal of the Royal College of General Practitioners*, 1984, 34, 146-9.

Henshaw, S.K., 'Induced Abortion: A World Review, 1990', *Family Planning Perspective*, 1990, 22 (2), 76-89.

Lloyd, J. and Laurance, K.M., 'Sequelae and Support after Termination of Pregnancy for Foetal Malformation', *British Medical Journal, Clinical Research Edition*, 1985, 290 (6472), 907-9.

Mattinson, J., 'The Effects of Abortion on Marriage', *Ciba Foundation Symposium*, 1985, 115, 150-64.

Ney Phillip, 'Relationship between Abortion and Child Abuse', *Canadian Journal of Psychiatry*, 1979, 24, 610-20.

Ney Phillip and Wickett, A.R., 'Mental Health and Abortion: Review and Analysis', *Psychiatric Journal of the University of Ottowa*, 1989, 14 (4), 506-16.

Rosenfeld, J.A., 'Emotional Responses to Therapeutic Abortion', *American Family Physician*, 1992, 45, 137-40.

Rue, Vincent M., *American Psychiatric Association, Diagnostic and Statistical Manual of Mental Disorders*, 1987.

Sim, Myre; and Neisser, Robert, 'Post-abortive Psychoses: A Report from Two Centres', *The Psychological Aspects of Abortion*, Washington, 1979, 14-24.

Speckhard, Anne C.; and Rue, Vincent M., 'Postabortion Syndrome: An Emerging Public Health Concern', *Journal of Social Issues*, 1992, 48 (1), 95-119.

SPUC Educational Research Trust, ed., Whelan, Robert, *Legal Abortion Examined: 21 Years of Abortion Statistics*, London 1992.

Torres, A.; and Forrest, J.D., 'Why do women have abortion?', *Family Planning Perspective*, 1988, 20 (4), 169-76.

Zolese, G. and Blacker, C.V.R., 'The Psychological Complications of Therapeutic Abortion', *British Journal of Psychiatry*, 1992, 160, 742-9.

One doctor's experience

MARGARET WHITE

In 1967, following the Steel Act which made abortion available more or less on demand with the aid of a pro-abortion doctor, I wondered how many patients I would lose because of my pro-life views. I was surprised to find that I lost none and even more surprised when I discovered that I acquired patients who had been aborted. Over the years I became experienced in treating Post-Abortion Syndrome.

I was not often asked for a letter of referral to hospital 'for a termination' (interesting euphemism!). On the few occasions when I was asked, I had little difficulty in refusing on legal grounds. I kept a copy of the Act in a drawer in my desk which I showed to these patients and asked which category their case came under. On no occasion could I swear 'in good faith' that the patient's physical or mental health would be more seriously harmed by the pregnancy than by the abortion. In most of these cases the reverse would have been true. In every case but one the patient went off to one of the 'cash clinics' and got their abortion. The patient who was the exception came back to see me a week after her request and said that she had changed her mind. So I gave her an appointment for our ante-natal clinic. At thirteen weeks she came to see me in great distress following a blood stained discharge and, through her tears, she said 'don't say this means I am going to lose my baby'. Happily her fears were unfounded but her changed reaction to the pregnancy illustrates the typical ambivalent attitude so often present in an early and 'unwanted' pregnancy.

In the early 1970s one of my registered patients, whom I had not seen before, came with a multitude of minor symptoms which denoted clinical depression. Her records showed nothing apart from a few childhood illnesses. She was not keen to talk about herself and only wanted pills to make her better. I discovered, however, that she had recently had an abortion in a London teaching hospital to which she had been referred by the student health service. She was not a student herself, but her lover was. Her main complaint was hair loss and insomnia but she was also anorexic and lethargic. Before I had a chance to comment on her condition she interjected with vigour 'don't you dare say that it has anything to do with my termination'. She came many times and always contested my diagnosis of a depressive state. Tests were done to exclude all the other conditions which might have produced similar symptoms—all were negative.

At that time she was one of the most difficult patients with whom I ever had to deal with. She was deeply unhappy, weeping, drinking too much, but still aggressively denying that she was depressed. I now know, but I didn't then, that this denial state is common. After about nine months she disappeared and I learnt that she had emigrated to Australia having broken with her lover some months before.

Two years later she came to see me again. She was still depressed. She had not been happy in Australia and was back in her old district. She told me that she had come to realise that my original diagnosis was right and asked me to help her. She was now quite a different person from the girl I had known two years before and was living at a different address, nearer to two other medical practices than to mine. I found it significant that she chose to come back to someone she knew to be a pro-life doctor.

It was much easier to help her now that she had passed through the denial stage. I believe there is an analogy here with alcoholism. Only when the patient can admit that they have a drink problem can it be successfully tackled. She responded to treatment and eventually regained her pre-abortion condition.

One of the saddest cases I have treated was a beautiful girl of twenty-one, tall, slim, self-assured, and beautifully dressed. She was involved in Haute Couture and engaged to be married in six months time. She asked for an abortion because she had an opportunity to advance her career at a fashion show in Paris two months later. When I suggested that she should get married a bit sooner she replied that an obviously pregnant woman, whether single or married, would not land the contract she hoped for. She was cheerful and friendly and easily recognised that the shape of one's abdomen at a Paris show was not an indication for an abortion under the Act.

About seven months later she came to see me with severe Post-Abortion Syndrome (PAS). She was not at all aggressive and realised herself that her weeping, anorexia, and insomnia were connected with her abortion. She was unable to work and came to see me every week. I asked her at one stage about her marriage plans. She told me that she had 'split up' with her fiancé. I was extremely sorry for her. She was thin, wan, and dressed drably. It was hard to believe that it was the same girl.

When she returned to work after several weeks I asked her during one of her visits about her career in the fashion world. She told me she had given it up and was working as a secretary. The result of 'the woman's right to chose' in her case was the loss of her health, her husband, and her job.

She was still coming to see me on a regular basis when I retired from the practice. She had lost all interest in the opposite sex. I did not probe into her personal life. I listened to what she wanted to talk about. If she had become sexually frigid I would not have been surprised because this is a fairly common symptom of PAS.

It is said that Queen Elizabeth I remained a virgin because, in her experience, marriage, as exemplified by her father, was associated with decapitation and this had naturally inhibited her libido.

Even those who make a lot of money out of doing abortions admit that having an abortion is an unpleasant experience. To connect the sexual act with an unpleasant experience tends to dampen the ardour. Sexual frigidity following abortion may be one of the reasons why the break up of the relationship with the father of the aborted child is common.

My first experience of PAS occurred before anyone realised that such a thing existed. It started in ignorance and ended in tragedy. With hindsight it is clear that the patient in question was a typical case. She was a woman in her early forties when I inherited her from my predecessor. She was what is known in the medical profession as a 'heart-sink' patient, because every time such a patient's face comes round the surgery door your heart sinks! She was deeply depressed but refused to admit it. She constantly quoted rare diseases she had read about in *Readers' Digest*, demanding to be tested for such conditions.

She had had an abortion in the more restricted times before the 1967 Act. It was performed by a London consultant in an expensive nursing home, so it couldn't be classed as a back-street abortion (so often proffered as a reason for unpleasant sequelae). The abortion was the result of an extra-marital affair while her husband was overseas for several months. There was no way she could pass off the child as his. This had been her first pregnancy and she never conceived again.

She was always tired, unable to concentrate, slept badly, and wept easily. Everything I tried failed. I wish I had been able to help her but the medical profession didn't know enough about the condition in those days.

One summer, twenty years after her abortion, she took her own life.

These are just three cases out of several I have treated. Three totally different women in class, intelligence, and personality. They all showed some typical aspects of PAS. Suicide is, of course, rare, but, in a study carried out at Westminster hospital on women who had attempted suicide, Dr Farmer reported that a significantly higher percentage of such patients had had an abortion than those of a control group.

PAS rarely comes on soon after the abortion. Women at this stage usually feel nothing but a sense of relief that they are now rid of their problem pregnancy. Alas! the majority do not realise that they will never be in the same state as they were before the pregnancy and abortion.

PAS usually comes on around the time when the child would have been born. Pro-abortion psychiatrists often quote surveys of post-abortion women showing that the abortion has had little effect on their mental health. These surveys, however, are mainly undertaken within three or four months of the operation and are valueless as they give a totally false picture of the emotional consequences of the abortion. The figures compiled by the government of the physical after effects are equally false and for the same reason because unless infection, bleeding, or other physical complications occur within a few days of the operation they will not usually be reported to the Department of Health.

In my practice I found that the second most common time for PAS to begin is after the birth of a woman's first living child. Several times I have heard it said 'only when I had my gorgeous baby did I realise what I did when I had my termination'.

The syndrome starts quite often with insomnia. My cases tended to suffer less from early waking than from difficulty in getting to sleep and waking during the night—often after a nightmare. Weeping is almost always present and occurs at random, sometimes causing embarrassment. Some patients are anorexic, some grossly over-eat. Only one of the women I treated admitted to over-drinking although this has been reported frequently by other doctors. Break-up of the relationship (even marriage) is very common. I found that this happens in most cases following abortion even when the patient does not suffer from PAS.

It often surprised me to find that patients whom I had refused to refer for abortion chose to come back and see me when they had problems. Several have said 'you're the only one who understands'. The significance of this could be rather sinister. It is possible that pro-abortion doctors do not wish to accept that there are any serious consequences arising from the operation and therefore treat the patients who have PAS as hysterics who are making a fuss. A spokesman for one of the largest abortion chains, in a moment of honesty, admitted that the most likely people to have depression after an abortion are those who had mental problems before the pregnancy. She warned that care must be taken before deciding to abort a woman with mental illness. Since nine out of ten abortions are allegedly performed because of the patient's actual (or reasonably foreseeable) mental health it is strange to be told that it is important for patients to be in a good state of mental health before an abortion!

Having treated many women with the physical complications of abortion I had believed, until the late seventies, that these were the main complications. However, over the last decade, it has become clear to me that for every one woman who has physical complications there are two or three who have emotional problems, and the treatment in these cases is long term, complicated, and time consuming.

Unresolved grief occurs frequently after both spontaneous and induced abortion. It is not sufficiently realised that every woman who has an abortion is the mother of a dead child. From the moment that the pregnancy is confirmed all women become aware of a second person within them. They may regret this presence or even hate and detest it, regarding it as an unwanted interloper, but though abortionists claim that the child in the womb is not a person, the mother herself knows this is untrue. This piece of dishonesty by abortionists has led to many of the feminist slogans so liberally used in demonstrations. Perhaps the commonest—'not the church and not the state, women must decide their fate'—shows this approach. A pregnant woman has decided her fate. Having an abortion won't alter the fact that she has been pregnant. Exactly the same applies to 'the woman's right to chose'. Unless she is one of those very rare cases where a woman becomes pregnant after rape, she *has* chosen—she chose to risk a pregnancy. The fact that she is able to get rid of her pregnancy emphasises the fact that what is in her womb is not just part of her body. If it were, women would spend most of their lives incomplete!

A review of the literature reveals that the incidence of PAS varies from 7% to 41%. Many of the papers on the subject which give a low incidence have been compiled, as already reported, on questions asked around three months after the abortion. The true PAS comes on slowly and insidiously, beginning somewhat later than this.

The government has done its best to push medical abortion with R.U.486 because it believes that this will be cheaper than surgical abortion. On the face of it an abortion produced by a pill and a pessary should be easier, safer, and the cause of less complications than a surgical operation. The latter involves the administration of an anaesthetic and the surgical invasion of a sterile part of the body both of which processes have a small but definite risk of later morbidity or even death. In spite of encouragement, medical abortion is not popular. This is fortunate for the mental health of our young women because there is little doubt that drug induced abortion will cause an increase in the incidence of PAS. Guilt is frequently present in women with this condition, though nearly always denied in the early stages.

In a surgical abortion a woman presents herself and is anaesthetised and by the time she wakes up someone else has killed her baby and disposed of its remains. In a medical abortion she herself must take the pills and insert the pessary and in many cases she sees the baby when she aborts. She cannot pass any responsibility onto another party and must carry its full weight on her own shoulders. It has already been reported that medical abortion increases the likelihood of PAS.

The ambivalent attitude of the public to abortion becomes clear in the method used to perform late abortions. The two methods of surgical and medical abortion are both used, but the surgical method now involves stretching the cervix considerably, inserting instruments much heftier than the suction catheter used in early abortions, and literally dismembering a small, wriggling baby. The medical method is, in fact, a premature induction of labour by means of drugs taken by mouth, pessary or injection. Doctors often object to the surgical method because, through their instruments, they can feel the baby moving, and dislike the process of placing all the dismembered pieces together to check that nothing has been left in the uterus. Patients do not like the second method because they must go through a form of labour, and a late miscarriage can be as painful as a normal labour, especially if it is drug induced. They must also feel the process of giving birth and may even see the baby, who on occasions, may be alive. This causes distress to the nurses as well as to the mother. The headline in an American journal of obstetrics and gynaecology some years ago read 'live birth main complication of mid trimester abortion'. Because of this 'complication' medical abortion usually includes a drug which ensures the birth of a dead baby.

The interesting fact about these two methods is that late abortions performed in National Health hospitals are usually medical and those done in private clinics are usually surgical. Is it possible to posit that some doctors will overcome their qualms about surgical late abortions if they are adequately compensated?

It is regularly alleged by pro-abortion feminists that any guilt which occurs after abortion is due to Christians 'forcing their morality' on the patient. In fact, none of my cases had any particular religious affiliation.

A fellow student of mine who was a confirmed atheist had an abortion in her last year at medical school. She had good social reasons. The father was in the forces overseas and the birth would have clashed with her final examinations. She married the father on his first leave and became pregnant again within the year and shortly after the birth of the child she took to drinking. The marriage ended in a divorce, by which time she was an alcoholic. Visiting her, some 30 years after her abortion, I was reminiscing happily about our six years together as students when she suddenly burst into tears and said 'I killed my baby, I killed my baby'. After comforting her I went out of the room and apologised to her second husband for having reminded her of her student days. 'It is not your fault' he replied, 'there is not a month goes by without those tears'.

Depression occurs in a small percentage of all maternities (this should not be confused with what is known as 'the baby blues', a weepy state coming on three or four days after delivery). It can be very distressing, but is more amenable to treatment than is PAS. In all my years of medical practice I have never come across a patient with puerperal depression which lasted more than a year, though I know that such cases do occur. I have encountered two cases of PAS lasting for over twenty years.

Abortion is essentially a family affair and involves the relationships between mother, father and child (or children). It takes two to make a baby, and for too long the father and any other children of the union have been ignored in the abortion decision. The mother, of course, is most at risk of physical and mental after-effects, but it is realised more and more that other members of the family also have problems arising from the abortion. In many cases a promiscuous youth will congratulate himself for 'gettting away with it' when his mistress has his child aborted, but there are other men who desperately want the child and suffer from having to stand by powerless while the fruit of their love is destroyed. As well as this loss they may have to endure an alteration in their lover. When we remember that women may become obese, anorexic, or alcoholic following an abortion, the effect on the father may be even more traumatic than he expected.

Children may also suffer, if they are aware that their mother has had a 'termination'. Most children long for an addition to the family that they can play with and brag about, and they are distressed when their mother miscarries; their distress may turn to resentment if they know that their loss was deliberately induced by their parents. Bad behaviour at school and even delinquency have been reported. It is well known that children frequently blame themselves when parents divorced; they may well also blame themselves for an abortion, thinking perhaps that their untidiness, or bad behaviour, was responsible for the fact that their mother couldn't face another child.

For a woman to overcome her abortion-induced depression she must clear her mind of cant and accept what she has done. Only by doing so can she overcome the conflict and confusion which is present. She had been told that abortion was as simple as having a tooth out and had no after effects. She believed this but unfortunately her body and mind did not. Trying to reconcile two irreconcilable facts causes serious mental confusion. Sometimes alcohol helps to numb the conflict, sometimes comfort eating does. Acceptance of the connection of the depression with the abortion is absolutely necessary for any cure to occur.

Once acceptance occurs, a cure can be expedited by some form of spiritual confession and absolution. Confession to a priest is not usually enough; some form of ritual is necessary (similar to the now hugely disused 'churching' of women after childbirth?). This can be arranged by both Muslim and Christian religions and all associations of victims of abortions have found it helpful. It is possible to have a short secular liturgical service of repentance and reconciliation for those women who do not wish for a religious one.

The state of pregnancy is an honourable estate as well as a miraculous one. Within hours of fertilisation the tiny embryo is sending messages to the endometrium ordering it to produce extra glucose because it is on its way down the fallopian tube to the uterus. Once there it will need the sugar to nourish it before it becomes fully embedded. At the same time messages are sent to the pituitary and back to the ovaries to prevent any further ovulation. This ban on ovulation lasts throughout pregnancy and lactation. The uterus is not an annexe to the body but is a part of it. Emptying the uterus by abortion does not alter the fact that the whole of the woman's body has been changed by the pregnancy to accommodate the developing child. The multitude of different hormones involved do not disappear like the dew in the morning just because the uterus is now empty.

Many of us have the misfortune to lose babies during pregnancy; it is a traumatic experience and recently it has been more generally recognised as such and special measures are now taken in hospitals to mitigate the suffering. Miscarriages are not of our doing, for some reason or other nature intervenes and ends the pregnancy.

Nature is conspicuously absent in the abortion chambers and it is a rare woman who has absolutely no after effects. Going against nature is always a risky business. We have only one body in this life. It is not a rehearsal body, we can't trade it in for a new one when we have made a mess of it. It is ours for life—we do well to take care of it.

There is an old saying that is still true: 'God always forgives, man sometimes forgives, but nature *never* forgives.'

Treatment of post-abortion syndrome

PATRICIA CASEY

CRITIQUE

This area of psychological intervention is not well developed for a variety of reasons. Predominantly it stems from the failure generally to recognise the psychological complications of induced abortion until recently. In addition, those who developed emotional consequences were reluctant to admit or recognise the likely precipitant, in a manner reminiscent of those traumatised by sexual abuse. Indeed, the medical profession omitted to investigate the psychological aspects of induced abortion for a variety of methodological as well as ideological reasons.

Studies of the psychological effects of induced abortion have often been methodologically flawed due to the assessment criteria for the disorder, to the questionnaires employed and to high drop-out rates. In consequence, rates for emotional disturbance varied between 0 and 40 per cent. In recent years, however, a number of methodologically sound studies have been forthcoming and point to a minimum prevalence for major depression and anxiety[1] of 10 per cent, although the exact figure is likely to be greatly in excess of this due to attrition,[2] to denial and to the time lag between the precipitant and the illness,[3] often running to five or more years. The knowledge of the high frequency of major psychiatric dysfunction following the procedure (a figure similar to that for post-natal depression) should lead to a more thorough investigation of psychological interventions for those suffering from the psychological complications of induced abortion.

1. G. Zolese and C.V.R. Blacker (1992), 'The psychological complications of therapeutic abortion', *British Journal of Psychiatry*, 160, 742-9.
2. N.E. Adler, (1967), 'Sample attrition of psychosocial sequelae of abortion. How qreat a problem?', *Journal of Applied Social Psychology*, 6, 240-59.
3. R. Kumar and K.M. Robson (1984), 'A prospective study of emotional disorders in childbearing women', *British Journal of Psychiatry*, 144, 35-47.

A further impediment to the development of such interventions has been the belief that reactions to stress, whether following personal injury, bereavement or other loss, are best managed using 'talking therapies' to the exclusion of medications. This has therefore limited the range of approaches and of assessments applied to the sufferers. Whilst some reactions to induced abortion can be treated using psychotherapeutic tools, in some patients intervention with anti-depressants is also appropriate.

It is proposed to adopt an eclectic approach to treatment in this chapter, although without the benefit of scientifically controlled outcome studies as are available in relation to psychiatric disorders with other precipitants.

RISK FACTORS FOR POST-ABORTION COMPLICATIONS

A number of factors have been identified as placing the patient at risk for long-term complications of abortion. These include coerced abortion, youth, having previous children, abortion for eugenic reasons,[4] poor relationship with mother[5] or partner,[6] ambivalence about the procedure, past psychiatric history, coming from a culture or sub-culture hostile to abortions and poor coping skills pre-operatively.

THE AIM OF THERAPY

Many patients coming to treatment will initially express dismay at the task in hand. Views such as 'but you can't undo what I've done' are commonplace. The importance of emphasising that the goal of treatment is to assist the patient to live with what has happened, rather than persuading her that it was 'all right' or that she should forget about it, is obvious. In particular, persuasion has no part to play and the approach is to assist the patient in dealing with the events and in reconciling herself to what has happened. A further goal of intervention is the reduction of distress, although this often increases during the early stages of therapy. Unlike some other patient groups, the acceptance of responsibility for decisions and actions taken is not an issue in this group and, indeed, self-blame is frequently a persistent feature.[7,4]

4. S. Iles and D. Gath (1993), 'Psychiatric outcome of termination of pregnancy for foetal abnormality', *Psychological Medicine*, 407-13.
5. E.C. Payne, A.R. Kravitz and M.T. Notman (1976), 'Outcome following therapeutic abortion', *Archives of General Psychiatry*, 33, 725-33.
6. S.P. Llewellyn and R. Pytches (1988), 'An investigation of anxiety following termination of pregnancy', *Journal of Advanced Nursing*, 13, 468-71.
7. B. Lask (1975), 'Short term psychiatric sequelae to therapeutic termination of pregnancy', *British Journal of Psychiatry*, 126, 173-7.

More general issues relating to relationships should also be addressed. In particular, problems of low self-esteem are often in evidence both before and to a greater extent after the abortion. The basis for this, in addition to techniques for dealing with confidence, will need to be explored. If the therapist does not have the necessary skills, then referral to a psychiatrist/psychologist who has, is important. In particular, training in assertiveness and problem solving techniques may be necessary, particularly if the patient has entered dominating relationships. Since up to 24 per cent of women having an abortion have a history of prior abortions, the importance of developing decision making skills is obvious.

DEALING WITH THE IMMEDIATE REACTIONS

The reactions to abortion can be grouped into two categories—those typical of grief and those which are specific to the pregnancy loss.

Grief reactions

Most women describe short-term distress and unhappiness following the abortion operation. For most such feelings pass within a few weeks without any specific intervention. For those whose reactions are more severe regular contact will be necessary. Help is most likely to be sought from a counsellor or doctor not connected with the provision of the abortion.[1] The frequency should initially be determined by the patient and may vary from every other day to every fortnight. These sessions are to provide an opportunity for the patient to ventilate emotions. The common feelings described are sadness, feelings of being alone, anger at the referring agent and service provider and guilt (see below). Time must be allowed in order to ventilate these feelings. Many sessions may thus be spent saying very little apart from the patient's own articulation of distress. If anger is the dominant feature, then this can be vented by verbalising it or by putting the feelings in writing.

If anger is directed at a parent, perhaps because of coercion, or at a partner, then the use of photographs, particularly if the patient has difficulty expressing it, can be helpful in stimulating emotional expression.

Similar to the approach used in treating other major traumas, exposure by recall is essential.[8] It is helpful also in the early stages of therapy to allow the patient to describe the events at the time of the operation, e.g. the journey to the clinic, the room in which the patient stayed and the feelings sourrounding these places and events. In this aspect of therapy, it is the emotional component which is therapeutic, although descriptions of places

---

8. E. Lindemann (1944), 'Symptomatology and management of acute grief', *American Journal of Psychiatry*, 50, 294-305.

and events will help to consolidate the therapeutic relationship. These descriptive sessions may take place over two or three contacts. Resistance to recall may be encountered and, indeed, some patients often default at this point. Collusion in denial places the patient at risk of more prolonged reactions.

Pregnancy loss reactions
Many patients will wonder what the baby would have looked like, will articulate questions about it's gender and size and, as a result, avoid reminders about babies. Thus a patient may avoid passing baby shops, will not meet friends with infants and may avoid television programmes when matters relating to pregnancy are being discussed. Inquiries and questions about the baby may intensify around the time of expected delivery[4] and, therefore, closer professional contact is needed during this period. The patient should be allowed to articulate these questions and many find it helpful to describe her beliefs about the baby's appearance. Since many are embarassed by these thoughts, the therapist should inquire sensitively about this, e.g. 'Did you ever wonder about whether your baby was a boy or a girl?' This will then afford the patient the opportunity to articulate other questions about the baby's appearance. Patients who have seen the aborted infant, as after an abortion for eugenic reasons, may wish to describe in detail aspects of the baby's appearance.

In the immediate aftermath of an abortion the presence of suicidal ideation should be ruled out using the standard questions about hopelessness, suicidal plans, wish-to-live versus wish-to-die. The patient's concept of the medical lethality of the method chosen should also be assessed. Of the upmost significance is the presence of supports and confidants for the patient. The presence of suicide intent is a pointer to the need for referral to the medical (if being seen by a counsellor) or psychiatric services for urgent assessment. Indeed, hospitalisation may on rare ocassions be necessary to prevent suicide.

Most will have dealt with the initial emotional reaction to induced abortion within three to six months. If symptoms persist for longer, then further treatments are necessary.

LONG-TERM REACTIONS

Long-term reactions vary in intensity and in presentation. The most common is unresolved guilt, which is not necessarily a psychiatric disorder *per se*, although in some patients it may be a symptom of depressive illness. Where it occurs without any depression, the basis for it should be explored in therapy. Persistent guilt is particularly prominent in those who have abortions for fetal abnormality[4] although it has been described in all groups. For some it may be guilt at having let down one's parents, for others a spiritual guilt related to beliefs about having taken life or being unworthy of God's forgiveness. The latter two are more appropriately dealt with by ministers of religion, and sometimes those who have no strongly held religious beliefs will request such help. When dealing with more general feelings of having let others down, the perceived expectations of others must be explored and the positive attributes of the patient identified.

Persistent guilt is also a feature of depressive illness and is the most common disorder following induced abortion. It will manifest itself as a persistent grief reaction which fails to resolve in spite of appropriate psychotherapy. Other features include sleep and appetite disturbance, impaired concentration, panic attacks and anhedonia (total loss of pleasure). These should be managed using a two-pronged approach of anti-depressants and psychotherapy, as described above. The development of new symptoms, particularly after the birth of a baby, either to the patient or to a close family member or friend also indicates a re-awakening of the mourning process. One study has pointed to the increased risk of depressive illness in early pregnancy in those who have had prior abortions;[3] and the onset of this will require exploration of the feelings about the abortion, the baby etc., as described earlier. Antidepressants will almost certainly be necessary, although the risks of using them in the first trimester of pregnancy must be counterbalanced by the severity of the illness and the degree of incapacity it induces.

Anxiety disorders are less common but also require treatment using anxiety management techniques and at times anti-depressants in addition to psychotherapy. Avoidance due to panic attacks may require specialised treatment, using exposure and cognitive therapy. Referral to specialist services must then be arranged.

Although most studies have found a low incidence of psychotic illness, one study has described the onset of psychotic symptoms following abortion.[9] For this, psychiatric treatment, often as an in-patient or less commonly as an out-patient, will be essential. Treatment with major tranquillizers will bring about symptomatic relief. Psychotherapy should be suspended and thereafter the approach should be one of support rather than exploration of emotions, since relapse of the psychosis may be precipitated.

9. H.B. David (1985), 'Post-abortion and post-partum psychiatric hospitalisation. In Abortion: Medical Progress and Social Implications', *CIBA Foundation Symposium*, 115, 150-61.

WHEN ARE ANTI-DEPRESSANTS REQUIRED?

In spite of the reluctance to consider anti-depressants in patients with post-abortion depression, it is likely that a two-pronged approach using both psychotherapy and medication will be necessary in some. There are no studies to point to the effectiveness of anti-depressants, although their benefit has been demonstrated both in post-traumatic stress disorder and depressive illness, even when precipitated by bereavement.

The distinction between a normal grief reaction and a delayed reaction is pertinent in this regard. Those who are still within the first 3-6 months of grieving are unlikely to require anti-depressants although the presence of anhedonia (pervasive loss of pleasure), of persistent sleep disturbance, preoccupation with the the loss and panic attacks should suggest the possibility of prescribing anti-depressants. Reactions which persist unabated after six months should also be considered for treatment with anti-depressants, in the first instance. Finally, those who are receiving psychotherapy but not responding, should also be considered for pharmacotherapy.

The symptom of pathological guilt, so helpful in the generality of depressed patients as a pointer to the necessity for anti-depressants, is largely unhelpful in this group since guilt is common[10] and decisions about what constitutes appropriate and pathological guilt are more likely to reflect the therapist's own convictions than those of the patient. However, a patient from a religious background who has received religious 'counselling' or been to confession and still describes intense feelings of being 'beyond salvation' or of 'being wicked' is likely to be pathologically guilty. It is essential that in assessing guilt, the therapist should take account of the patient's background and steps that have been taken previously to alleviate it. On no account should the therapist express a view about the patient's culpability or otherwise.

Once anti-depressants are prescribed, there is little to be gained by continuing with psychotherapy, until a full response to them has been achieved. The patient will be unable to deal with the intense emotions generated during sessions and response to the anti-depressants may be compromised. Once a response has ocurred, then formal psychotherapy can resume.

In view of the association between depression in early pregnancy and a history of prior abortion,[3] caution must be exercised in prescribing anti-depressants in the first trimester. Thereafter they can be prescribed in accordance with manufacturers guidelines. For the lactating woman tricyclic

---

10. H.S. Greer, S. Lal and S.C. Lewis (1976), 'Psychological consequences of therapeutic abortion. King's termination study III', *British Journal of Psychiatry*, 128, 74-9.

anti-depressants can be given although the newer SSRI group are not recommended due to lack of information.

GROUP THERAPHY/SELF-HELP

Although there is no information on the benefits or otherwise of self-help for this patient group, some women express the belief that they are alone in their suffering and anecdotal reports suggest that self-help groups aid in alleviating this. Group therapy should never be recommended until individual therapy with the patient has indicated improvement in the patient's distress, functioning and guilt. As with all groups, the aim should be exploration of emotions with a view to reducing distress. Care must be taken to avoid excessive dependency, since this will impede the recovery process; and ultimately the patient should be enabled to leave the group. If symptoms of depression, guilt and anxiety persist in the group setting after a period of several months, then the possibility that the group is reinforcing the negative emotions must be considered and advice given to withdraw—advice which may be resisted. Groups which emphasise guilt and sin are likely to be unhelpful.

REACTIONS DURING THERAPY

The development of distress is almost universal during sessions and this often increases, initially. Patients may desist from therapy at this time. Provided suicidal ideation does not supervene, treatment should continue. Should the patient become suicidal then medical assessment is necessary. The development of depressive illness, as described above, warrants the temporary suspension of treatment and the initiation of anti-depressants. The patient may show an increase in the level of distress around the time of estimated delivery, if the pregnancy had continued, and extra support is necessary at this time.

During therapy some women will make attempts to become pregnant again, specifically to replace the 'lost' infant or to expiate guilt. Those who are unmarried may become promiscuous, whilst those in long-term relationships may avoid taking their usual contraceptive precautions. The desire to become pregnant again may or may not be articulated by the patient. Some may be encouraged to become pregnant by their partner, especially if he opposed the abortion. This, however, should be actively discouraged until the grief has abated.

WORKING WITH PARTNERS

After abortion the relationship between the patient and her partner often deteriorates and decisions may be made either to separate or to marry (if unmarried). As in dealing with any crisis, personal and relationship decisions should be delayed as far as is practical.

Specifically, marital therapy may be required when disparate views about the abortion lead to conflict. More commonly, however, the partner fails to acknowledge the emotional difficulties the woman is experiencing and therapeutic input may be necessary to explain this and give advice on ways of handling it. The partner may himself be distressed if the abortion occured for eugenic reasons and he may need individual therapy. This is likely to be of shorter duration than that required by the woman and he is likely to improve spontaneously once her well-being improves.

SPIRITUAL MATTERS

The spiritual aspects of abortion are not within the remit or competence of the author. However, some basic guidelines are important in considering this aspect of abortion. Surprisingly, many women from religious backgrounds do not seek or wish to obtain spiritual guidance following abortion. Even more surprising is the fact that many who are not committed to any religious group do request help from religious sources. In therapy this decision depends exclusively on the wishes of the patient. It is important that therapists and doctors working in this field, irrespective of their own religious beliefs, have access to a number of ministers of religion. Not only is access important, but the approach adopted by individuals may help or impede the process of treatment.

Some women express regret that they have let 'God' down and will describe an inability to pray or even visit a church. Putting these feelings in writing, perhaps in the form of a letter to God, can be most helpful in advancing this aspect of the treatment process and, unlike the more specifically religious aspects, can be conducted by the therapist. Not only is it necessary to write the feelings but also to read/articulate these in order to externalise them. This is unlikely to be possible or successful until a good working relationship has been established and a spirit of trust exists between patient and therapist.

Many women seek a commemoration ceremony for the infant and whilst this may seem macabre to those not working in this area, it is indicative of a positive response to treatment. A name may be chosen also and sometimes family members who are sympathetic attend. As with other aspects of the trauma of abortion, a ceremony should not be imposed and occurs only at the behest of the woman. Again a sensitive minister of religion is vital if this ritual is to be therapeutic.

CONCLUSION

There is little scientific information on the most appropriate models of intervention in those who suffer the psycholoqical complications of abortion. Those working in this area are advised to use models of treatment used in other forms of bereavement and major trauma. It is essential that this dearth of information be rectified by properly conducted studies of treatment.

Relationship between induced abortion and child abuse and neglect: four studies*

PHILIP G. NEY, TAK FUNG,
ADELE ROSE WICKETT

Abstract: Four studies designed to investigate between induced abortion and child abuse found a number of positive correlations. These findings appear to run counter to popular opinion and some professional declarations that making abortion freely available would terminate unwanted children and thus lower the incidence of child mistreatment. There is no evidence that the incidence of child abuse has declined with more readily available abortion. We found unwanted children were not more often abused, but that women who had previous pregnancy losses were more likely to abuse or neglect their children. There are a number of possible explanations for this, but the one which most closely fits the data is that pregnancy losses, particularly abortion, tend to make a women more anxious during a subsequent pregnancy, and more depressed after the child is born. The anxiety and depression interfere with the parent–infant bonding process, thus leaving a child more exposed to periods when the parents are unconcerned about his/her needs or are enraged by irritating behaviour. Mothers who physically or verbally abuse their children tend to react with anger to the infant's cry. Those who neglect their children tend to react with anxiety or feelings of helplessness. We also found that women not supported by their partners are more likely to miscarry or terminate a pregnancy. Lack of support by husbands and lack of breast-feeding also appear to contribute to abuse and neglect. It is possible that husbands are less supportive because they fear that their infants might be aborted and they are powerless to stop it.

*This article first appeared in *Pre- and Perinatal Psychology Journal*, 8(1), Fall 1993, and is reproduced with the kind permission of the Pre- and Perinatal Psychology Association of North America.

INTRODUCTION

Some authorities (Calef, 1972; Dennis, 1976; Greenland, 1973) have contended that every child should be a wanted child, partly because of a belief that unwanted children are more likely to be abused and neglected The thought was that elective abortion of unwanted children would help prevent child mistreatment. Now that western society provides effective contraceptives and abortion on request, nearly every child is 'wanted'. Remarkably few studies have been found that compare the incidence of child abuse and neglect today to earlier periods. However, although there appears to be some dispute as to whether or not there is an increase in the incidence of mistreatment or an improvement in reporting, it seems to be that the former is the case. Knudson (1988) of Purdue University studied the reports to a child protection agency over a 20-year period, and concluded that their growth reflects a genuine increase in abusive and neglectful behaviour. The reports corroborate earlier findings that child mistreatment has increased (Fontana and Bersharov, 1977; Kempe and Helfer, 1972; Bergstrand et al., 1979). These findings have necessitated a revaluation of the hypothesis that abortion prevents child abuse. We are investigating an alternative hypothesis: that readily available abortion is contributing to an increase in child abuse and neglect.

LITERATURE SURVEY

There appears to be an association between the rates of child abuse and abortion (Ney, 1979). Canadian provinces that have high rates of abortion also have high rates of child abuse the rates have increased parallel to each other. In British Columbia the rates of death of children and adolescents from social causes seem to have increased shortly after the change in legislation liberalising abortion (Tonkin, 1979). Although this association may be due to common causes such as socioeconomic conditions or social attitudes towards children, it is clear that there is no evidence that there has been a diminution in the rate of abuse.

The central issues for the medical profession with respect to physician-induced abortion are: 'Is it therapeutic?', i.e., is it effective in treating some disease or disorder? and 'Is it safe?', i.e., does it do more good than harm? Although there have been many attempts to demonstrate that abortion is safe, there has been almost no research done to determine its effectiveness in treating medical, psychological, or social illnesses. There is growing evidence that abortion does more harm than good as a medical procedure (Ney, 1989). One of the dangers of abortion may be that it disrupts future parent–infant bonding, We have been exploring the hypothesis that elective abortion and child abuse have a reciprocal positive correlation, and possibly a causal relationship.

Growing evidence indicates that any phenomenon that interferes with the early attachment of the mother to the child may be an important contributor to the pathogenesis of child abuse (Martin, 1976; Egeland and Sroufe, 1981), even in monkeys (Troisi et al., 1989). The first few critical hours of mother-infant contact can be interfered with if the mother is depressed (Colman and Colman, 1971). Some women become depressed on the anniversary of their abortion (Cavenar et al., 1978). Some women, although denying conflict immediately following the abortion, have severe conflicts that surface during psychotherapy (Kent et al., 1978) or during a subsequent pregnancy (Kumar and Robinson, 1978). According to some authors, 'the more motherly and more mature' women appear to feel post-abortion guilt (Herrenkohl and Herrenkohl, 1979; Pare and Hermione, 1970).

One third of mothers with children diagnosed as having failed to thrive are mourning the loss of a close relative. If one twin dies, the mother has difficulty attaching to the survivor (Klaus and Kennell, 1976). The death of a close friend, an earlier abortion or loss of previous children may delay preparation for the infant and retard bond formation (Colman and Colman, 1971). Pregnant women who had a previous abortion (Bradley, 1984) were anxious during the pregnancy and depressed following the birth more often than those who had no previous abortion. Though longer and more intense mourning was seen in mothers for whom pregnancy was a positive experience, mothers grieved whether an infant lived one hour or twelve days, whether it weighed 3,000 grams or a nonviable 580 grams, and whether the pregnancy was planned or unplanned (Klaus and Kennell, 1976). Findings indicate that grief is not significantly related to birth weight or duration of the life of the dead infant (Benfield, 1978). Parents have difficuly adjusting to the loss of their newborn (Culberg, 1971). Although there is considerale controversy regarding the amount of grief experienced by women who have induced abortions, it is agreed that women and spouses who have elected to abort their wanted but handicapped children experience measurable grief in 70 to 90 per cent of the instances. It has been reported to be important to later parenting whether or not the death of a stillborn is mourned (Lewis, 1979). It has long been recognised that a significant personal loss without complete mourning interferes with subsequent attachments (Bowlby, 1960; Freud, 1917). Children and adults have difficulty developing bonds with those who replace lost loved ones. The arguments and evidence advanced in 1979 (Ney, 1979) obviously needed further investigation. Although not the only object of our studies of child mistreatment (Ney and Herron, 1985; Ney et al., 1986; Ney, 1987; 1988a; 1988b; Ney et al., 1992) we have uncovered reasonably convincing evidence to support the original hypothesis that abortion tends to increase rather than decrease the likelihood of child abuse and neglect

CLINICAL CASE

Mrs G., a 23-year-old teacher's aide, was seen with her husband because she screamed incessantly at her five-year-old son, threw him violently onto the bed, hit him until there were red marks and nearly strangled him. Her father (a sergeant in the army) and her mother were described as being very patient: 'We were never spanked or screamed at.' Her parents later divorced. At the age of seventeen she began seeing a psychiatrist. She was sexually active from an early age, and at seventeen she became pregnant. Her parents and her physicians felt that she should have an abortion. She wanted a child but did not want to further upset her parents. She felt like running away. Following the abortion she seemed to be in a better state. However, her subsequent psychiatric course was stormy, with frequent overdoses. When she later married and became pregnant she was excited. She had persistent fears of losing the pregnancy and therefore refused intercourse. The infant was 9.5 lbs at birth and spent a short period in intensive care.

The mother was perplexed at her reaction to the child: 'As soon as they handed me the baby, I handed him back. It was a weird sensation. I was excited about having a baby, but it didn't work out. I had to prop the bottle when feeding him. I couldn't touch him.' Although she was given a great deal of support at home, she was so anxious that she could not eat and was placed on tranquilisers. She began screaming and hitting her baby, tossing him violently onto the bed and desperately trying to stop his crying: 'I used to get pissed off when he cried. I never felt close, not as much as I thought I would.' This woman had happily anticipated having a child and felt that she would be confident in handling him. She had no difficulty with her nieces and nephews, who frequently cried. She concluded: 'If I had had the first child, I would not have been frightened and wouldn't have had this problem.'

The child and parents were treated in a child psychiatric unit. Now the mother feels more confident in handling the child but still has frightening dreams of her baby drowning. She suddenly sits up in bed with a soundless scream. She still finds it difficult to look into the eyes of the child and he seldom makes eye contact with her. She is determined to tell no one about her next pregnancy in case someone tries to pressure her into an abortion.

STUDY 1

Methodology

One hundred known child-abusing mothers from the practice of two child psychiatrists and two Parent in Crisis groups were matched with nonabusing mothers. Each group was given a 59-item questionnaire covering factors related to child abuse. The children were also interviewed to determine their awareness of any factors that might influence their parent's attitude toward them. A subsequent study will follow the second pregnancy of women who aborted their first baby compared to a matched group of mothers whose first pregnancy ended in a live birth, to determine the rates of abuse in both groups. The children of mothers who have had abortions will be followed to determine the rate of child abuse in their offspring.

Results

The 100 randomly selected abused children in this study had different histories:
58 — excessive physical punishment (spanked more than twice a week);
30 — Physical assault leaving discernible marks;
15 — mental abuse producing depression in the child;
9 — sexual assault, all by males;
6 — neglect or abandonment;
18 — a combination of abuse;
9 — children were known prematures;
6 — adopted.

Of a subsample of 12 families randomly selected and more intensively studied, six children had experienced excessive physical punishment, three were assaulted, three were verbally abused, one child was premature and one was in an incubator for 11 days. Though five were not wanted at the beginning of the pregnancy, all were wanted babies at the time of delivery.

The mothers of these 12 children had previous losses, five had abortions, six had miscarriages, one had a stillbirth, and two had both abortions and miscarriages. Seven of the first pregnancies ended in miscarriage, stillbirth or abortion. Four of the 12 women had been abused as children and five were depressed postpartum. Of the three women whose first pregnancies were aborted, two were depressed postpartum, one had been abused with excessive punishment, and three had assaulted the referred child. The mother of one of these women had an infant who died, while another had a stillbirth. Though there was no correlation between the miscarriages of individual mothers and grandmothers, it was noted that seven maternal grandmothers had a miscarriage, stillbirth or infant death. The control group, selected from mothers of children with severe emotional or behavioural disorders that were hospitalised in the Child and Family Psychiatric Unit of the Royal Jubilee Hospital, Victoria, BC, was matched for age (EG 19-37 yr. average 22 yr. cf. CG 18-25 yr. average 25 yr) and perfectly so for marital status and socioeconomic status (EG 3.7 cf. CG 3.5). The control group mothers had one abortion reported. This was significantly fewer on a 1-tailed test, $Z=1.70< .05$. The control group had four miscarriages or stillbirths, $Z=1.25$ and not significantly different from the sample studied.

STUDY 2

Methodology

One hundred and sixty-two children and 206 adults are the present sample of an ongoing study of child abuse and neglect. The study is predominantly clinical, involving private practice, child psychiatric units, and a young offenders centre, but it also includes a sample of volunteers from a local high school and the parents of those who have brought their children for psychiatric evaluation and treatment. Measures were made with the use of the Child Experience Questionnaire, devices that have established reliability and validity (Ney et al., 1986; Ney, 1987). Visual analogue scales were used to assess the frequency and severity of physical abuse, verbal abuse, sexual abuse, physical neglect and emotional and intellectual neglect. Measures were made of the age of onset, the duration, the impact on the child, of how abnormal it was felt to be and of various effects it had on self-perception and perception of life.

Results

Table 1 indicates a significant association between the number of losses experienced by the mother and the chance that she will more severely abuse one of her children.

Table 1: Pregnancy Losses* and Child Abuse

Extent of Abuse to Child	Mother Has Experienced Loss(es)	Mother Has Experienced No Loss	
More severe abuse	(61.7%) 21	(32.2%) 13	(100%) 33
Less severe abuse	(33.3%) 9	(66.7%) 18	(100%) 27
No abuse	(23.1%) 6	(76.9%) 20	(100%) 26

*Losses are defined as miscarriages, induced abortions and stillbirths.
Total N = 87 $X^2 = 10.136$ df = 2   p = 0.007

To determine whether the bonding between parent and child might be interfered with by losses or by type of birthing, we examined the birthing experiences of mothers in the Christchurch Women's Hospital in New Zealand and those who delivered at home. It appears that there was no significant difference with how pleased they were with the birth, or with how much pain they experienced. Although there was some difference in how soon they held their baby, there was no appreciable difference in the mean rate of bonding. We assessed how much the mother wanted the child who was being studied; before being pregnant, early in the pregnancy, late in the pregnancy and after the child's birth. We found there was a significant change in wanting (Table 2). It also appears (Fig. 1) that abusing mothers are more likely to want their child. Table 3 indicates the results of the step-wise regression analysis of the sixty-four factors we considered might possibly contribute to child mistreatment. It appears that the lack of breast-feeding and lack of support from husbands most closely correlate with the extent of abuse and neglect. It also appears that the mother's ability to breast-feed is related both to her inclination to touch the child and to the child's cuddliness. The effect on the mother of the infant's cry appears to be either that of anxiety and helplessness resulting in neglect of the child, or anger resulting in physical or verbal abuse.

STUDY 3

Methodology
A long-term study of 1265 children born in Christchurch, New Zealand in 1977 has produced a great deal of information about the family life, health, and social circumstances of these children (Fergusson et al., 1989). The

Table 2: Changes in 'Wantedness'

	Mother Wants Child			
	very much	unsure	not at all	
When first pregnant	(73.1%)	(15.4%)	(11.5%)	(100%)
	76	46	12	104
At birth	(89.6%)	(3.8%)	(6.6%)	(100%)
	95	54	7	106
Now	(91.0%)	(0.0%)	(9.0%)	(100%)
	80	0	8	89

$X^2 = 22.86$ df = 4 $p < 0.001$

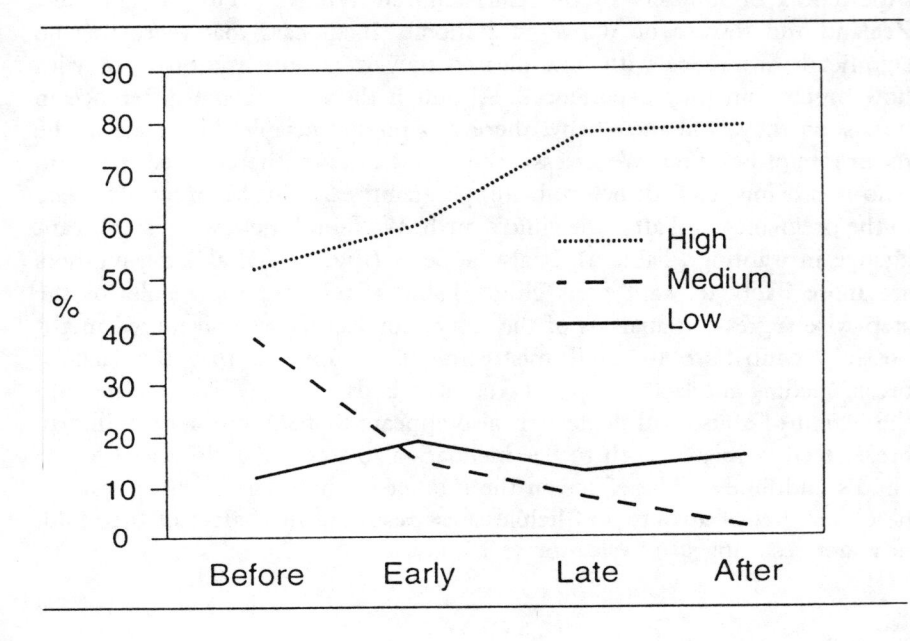

Figure 1: Abusing mothers who want pregnancy
(horizontal axis shows period of pregnancy)

Table 3: Causes of Abuse and Neglect

Physical abuse	Verbal abuse	Physical neglect	Emotional neglect	Sexual abuse
Lack of breast feeding*	Husband not supportive	Husband not home	Breast feeding not enjoyable	Affected by abortion loss
Husband not home during pregnancy	Breast feeding not enjoyable	Affected by death of spouse or close friend	Husband not supportive during childhood	Number of abortions
	Fear of losing pregnancy			Breast feeding not enjoyable

*Length of breast feeding determined mostly by: 1) how enjoyable, 2) quality of touch (initial reaction).
Rank ordered from stepwise regression analysis.

Christchurch Child Development Study has conducted home interviews, collected questionnaires, and added data from the records of hospitals, public health agencies, and private practitioners. Studies have been made at the time of birth, and at the ages of four months, one year, two years, three years, and four years of age. As part of this study, mothers were questioned about various aspects of their pregnancies and child-raising experiences. The results are significant in highlighting some aspects of both child abuse and abortion.

Results

The women in this study who had experienced an abortion were much more likely to have experienced a number of traumatic life-events, such as moves, death of someone close to them, or accidents (Chi square, $p < 0.0000$).

Mothers were interviewed and asked to report their emotional reactions to having lost a child through a miscarriage, abortion, stillbirth, or adoption. It appears that the longer the pregnancy involvement with the child, the more the mothers were bereaved following their loss. However, women still grieved the loss of a child by abortion to a greater extent than those lost by miscarriage, even though the abortions were done earlier in the gestation (Table 4). Women who were assaulted by their husbands were found to be more likely to abuse their children than mothers whose husbands did not assault them ($p < 0.038$). The incidence of child abuse was not higher in pregnant mothers, even though they are presumably under greater stress than nonpregnant women ($p < 0.309$).

Table 4: Residual Emotional Effects of Pregnancy Loss

Residual grief	Type of pregnancy loss			
	Miscarriage	*Abortion*	*Stillbirth*	*Adoption*
Still bereaved	15.0%	24.4%	40.0%	41.8%
Not bereaved	85.0%	75.8%	60.0%	58.2%

Interestingly, there was little correlation between those mothers who used occasional physical discipline on their children (for example, a 'smack'), and those who abused them. That is, the abusive mothers were generally not the same ones who used corporal discipline in a moderate fashion ($p < 0.290$).

A number of factors: e.g., employment, number of toys, frequency of trips outside the home, kindergarten attendance, etc., were lumped together to measure the amount of 'social disadvantage' experienced by children.

Sixty-one percent of the abused children fell into the category of the highest social disadvantage. Families of the socially disadvantaged were more likely to be single-parent families who had a significant history as abused children.

As table 5 demonstrates, there are five significant Spearman Correlation Coefficients between a previous abortion and the severity of abuse or neglect. Other correlations with abuse did not reach statistical significance.

Table 5: Previous Abortion and Child Abuse

Type of abuse	Correlation	Significance
Severity of verbal abuse by mother	0.308	$p < 0.03$
Severity of physical abuse by mother	0.308	$p < 0.03$
Severity of emotional neglect by mother	0.265	$p < 0.05$
Severity of emotional neglect by father	0.405	$p < 0.00$
Severity of sexual abuse by father	0.345	$p < 0.01$

*Spearman Correlation Coefficients

STUDY 4

Methodology

With the assistance of the College of Family Physicians, we were able to provide a questionnaire to women of child-bearing age or later who were waiting to see their family physicians. The questionnaire was handed out and collected by the receptionist. These women did not appear to differ, in terms of age, marital status, or number of children, from the general female population when compared to data from *Statistics Canada*. A sample of 1432 provided usable responses from the offices of 69 physicians. The visual analogue subjective estimates of the mothers' health correlated well with that of the independent observer and that of the family physician.

Results

It appeared that pregnancy losses have a cumulative negative effect on the mothers' general health (Table 6). Of these pregnancy losses, abortions had the most important negative impact (Table 7). Of the 44 factors we considered as affecting health, it appears the greatest contribution to poor general health was poor family life. The top three factors most seriously affecting the mother's present health are: poor family life, loss of the first pregnancy and poor partner support (Table 8).

Table 9 indicates that mothers are more likely both to abort and miscarry first or second pregnancies if they have insufficient partner support, and these factors continue to be important for five pregnancies (Table 10).

Table 6: Negative Effect of Pregnancy Losses* on Mother's Health

Number of losses	Pearson correlation* coefficient	Significance
1 Loss	0.018	p < 0.497
2 Losses	0.083	p < 0.002
3 Losses	0.104	p < 0.000

*Pregnancy losses include miscarriages, abortions, stillbirths, ectopic pregnancies, and early infant deaths

Table 7: Negative Influences on Mother's Present Health

Related factors	My present health is not good	
No. of full term normal birthweight	0.034	p < 0.194
No. of prematures	0.013	p < 0.194
No. of miscarriages	0.064	p < 0.041
No. of abortions	0.107	p < 0.000
No. of stillbirths	0.022	p < 0.403
No. of infant deaths	0.029	p < 0.268
Older age of mother	0.005	p < 0.860
Partner not supportive	0.263	p < 0.000

Expressed as Pearson Correlation Coefficients   N = 1428

Table 8: Principal Negative Influences on Mother's Present Health

	T	Significance
Poor family life	4.594	p = 0.0000
Loss of 1st pregnancy	2.838	p = 0.0048
Unsupportive partner	2.478	p = 0.0137

Expressed as a multiple regression

Table 11 shows the effect of immediacy (i.e. suddenness and realness of a startling quality), on a women's perceived need to obtain professional help for her pregnancy loss. Approximately 20 per cent feel a moderate or strong need for help in dealing with the loss.

Table 12 displays the correlations between the outcomes of the first and second pregnancies. Women tend to have repeated miscarriages and abortions. There is a 1.6 increase in second-pregnancy miscarriages if the first

Table 9: *Effect of Partner's Presence and Support on the Outcome of the First and Second Pregnancies*

Pregnancy outcome	Partner support					
	First pregnancy			Second pregnancy		
	Present and supportive	Present not supportive	Absent	Present and supportive	Present not supportive	Absent
Full term, normal birthweight	76.3	47.1	55.3	78.6	62.7	46.8
Full term, low birthweight	4.0	8.8	1.6	5.4	6.7	9.7
Premature	4.7	6.9	7.3	5.3	8.0	12.7
Miscarriage	8.7	18.6	8.9	7.8	12.0	9.7
Abortion, induced	4.0	16.7	25.2	1.1	8.0	19.4
Stillborn	1.1	1.0	0.8	0.5	0.0	1.5
Early infant death	0.8	0.0	0.0	1.0	2.7	0.0
Ectopic	0.3	1.0	0.8	0.3	0.0	0.0
	100%	100%	100%	100%	100%	100%
Combined abortion & miscarriage	12.7	35.7	34.1	8.9	20.0	29.1
		N = 969			N = 764	

X^2 significance = 0.0000

Table 10: *Significance of Age and Partner Support for Pregnancy Losses*

Factor influencing outcome	Pregnancy number					
	1st	2nd	3rd	4th	5th	6th
Age	116.607 p < 0.000	78.541 p < 0.000	32.374 p < 0.054	19.212 p < 0.379	20.571 p < 0.648	9.631 p < 0.648
Partner present and supportive	106.503 p < 0.000	86.286 p < 0.000	78.768 p < 0.000	60.275 p < 0.000	27.638 p < 0.006	5.577 p < 0.694
Partner at birth	2.892 p < 0.895	1.407 p < 0.965	33.545 p < 0.000	0.185 p < 0.999		

Expressed as Chi-Squares

Table 11: *Effect of the Immediacy of a Pregnancy Loss* on the Mother's Need for Professional Help*

Mother's need	Loss in first pregnancy	Loss in first and last pregnancies	Loss in last pregnancy
No need for professional help	80.9	64.9	67.4
↓	6.6	9.6	3.5
	1.6	8.8	5.8
	0.5	2.6	1.2
	5.5	7.9	5.8
	2.2	0.9	5.8
	0.5	4.4	1.2
Need help a great deal	1.1	0.9	4.7
	1.1	0.0	4.7
	100% N = 183	100% N = 114	100% N = 86

Pearson's R = 0.75409 p < 0.0000
X^2 = 391.21614 p < 0.0000
*Losses defined as miscarriages, stillbirths and abortions

one is aborted. Table 13 is a summary of the first (most significant) five factors which appear to determine if the third pregnancy will end in a full-term baby or is lost. It also appears that if their abortions are not included in the tally, young women are as likely to have as many full-term healthy pregnancies as are mature women.

DISCUSSION

It appears that there is a complex relationship between abortions and child abuse. It is possible that a mother who has had an abortion is more anxious during the next pregnancy and more depressed postpartum. Consequently, she is less able to bond with her next child. It is also possible that abortion interferes with the mother's general health, giving her less of the emotional freedom and physical vigour needed to care for the dependent infant.

It is possible that the abortion alters the mother's innate response to the infant's cry. Abortion may make it difficult for the mother to touch the baby, lessening the chance of breast-feeding and a healthy child. A less nourished child will cry more often and more pathetically, making the mother more anxious and/or irritable in her response to her infant's needs. It is also possible that wanted children are more likely to be abused because of the parents' higher expectations. The greater chance of being disappointed

Table 12: Relationship between First and Second Pregnancy Outcomes

The second pregnancy ends in:	Full term, N.B.W.	Full term, Low B.W.	Premature	Miscarriage	Abortion	Stillborn	Early death	Ectopic
Full term, normal birthweight	76.9	55.9	45.2	61.0	51.4	58.3	80.0	60.0
Full term, low birthweight	3.5	17.6	4.8	5.9	9.3	0.0	0.0	0.0
Premature	4.0	8.8	33.3	4.2	2.8	25.0	0.0	20.0
Miscarriage	9.3	8.8	14.3	21.2	14.0	16.7	20.0	20.0
Abortion	4.6	2.9	0.0	5.9	21.5	0.0	0.0	0.0
Stillborn	0.4	2.9	2.4	1.7	0.9	0.0	0.0	0.0
Early infant death	1.1	2.9	0.0	0.0	0.9	0.0	0.0	0.0
Ectopic	0.4	0.0	0.0	0.0	0.0	0.0	0.0	0.0
	100% N = 571	100% N = 34	100% N = 42	100% N = 118	100% N = 107	100% N = 12	100% N = 5	100% N = 5

$X^2 = 176.58424 \ p < 0.0000$

Table 13: Factors Affecting the Outcome of the Third Pregnancy

Full term	Loss
1. Partner generally supportive	1. Health affected by previous loss
2. Health not affected by previous loss	2. Partner not supportive during third pregnancy
3. Partner supportive during second pregnancy	3. Partner not generally supportive
4. Partner supportive during third pregnancy	4. Partner not supportive during second pregnancy
5. No previous pregnancy losses	5. Loss of first pregnancy

Note: Logistic regression

increases the parents' tendency to become enraged at children. All these factors seem to be related to the common denominator, lack of partner support.

Perhaps there is lack of partner support in the current social climate partly because the partner is not sure that the pregnancy with this child will continue. Knowing that his wife might independently decide to abort the infant, he does not attach himself to the infant or support the mother during the pregnancy. Evidence from our Pregnancy Out-come Study involving more than 1400 women shows that lack of partner support is the most significant variable leading to an increased tendency to abortion or spontaneous miscarriage. Evidence from another study indicates that approximately 80 per cent of the relationships examined break up following an abortion. We collected that data from a large post-abortion counselling service. This study of clients of a telephone counselling service also supports the observations of others that women who were sexually abused as children are more likely to seek abortions.

Although there are many possible explanations for the apparent connection between abortion and child abuse, it is possible that all these factors add to that relationship. However, if the parent-infant bonding is the main factor that is affected by abortion, it should be remembered that although bonding protects an infant from the parents' occasional episodes of rage or neglect, it is not absolute protection. Parents will only care for the bonded infant as well as they care for themselves and for each other.

Young mammals and many birds have an instinctual form of special attachments to parents, now known as bonding. This bond ensures contact, and contact has survival value. As long as there is contact, there is an optimal chance of being directed towards food and away from danger. Because the bond is generally exclusive to the parents, it provides protection from some other adult or other species known to steal the young from the parents. The immature offspring react to strange adults as if they were possible predators. These mechanisms to ensure care and to avoid predatory strangers are essential for the survival of any species. And the human child is bonded to its parent for the same reasons. Children who do not have a parent-exclusive bond will more readily accept the seductive attention of strangers.

It has been observed that when a stranger visited a daycare centre where a low partition divided visitors from the children, at least seven or eight children came to the partition and lifted up their hands expectantly, wanting to be picked up. It appeared that they had few inhibitions about being taken away. Under normal conditions the child would shy away from a stranger and scream if picked up by one. The child who does not have this built-in defence is more vulnerable to abduction or sexual assualt.

The parent-infant bond is quite durable but it can be broken. In one modern daycare they carefully constructed a sound-attenuating room where the child would be left to cry by itself when its mother left. This is so he or she would not disturb the other children or, more particularly, the daycare workers. According to the operator, it takes six or seven days for the child to 'adjust' to being without its parents and to stop crying. In addition to breaking the special bond, this crying room is able to teach a child that the pain of his or her loss will not be attended to, no matter how desperately he or she expresses anger, fear or sorrow.

Since the parent-infant bond is so necessary to the nurture and survival of children, it is important to study any effect that might be promoted by a social change in parenting. Abortion has now been experienced by between 50 per cent (Forrest, 1987) and 70 per cent (Ney, 1983) of North American women by the time they reach age 45. Even if it had a small effect on each individual, it could have a large impact on the overall incidence of child abuse and neglect. There is a remarkable degree of agreement between the studies we have done in separate cities with different populations. The initial hypothesis that there is a positive rather than negative relationship between child abuse and abortion (Ney, 1979) is holding up after fourteen years of collecting and analyzing data. A Medline database search shows no substantial evidence to the contrary. Our studies, although not conclusive, seem to indicate that there is an important relationship between abortion and child abuse that must be studied further. Those who recommend therapeutic terminations should consider this possibility.

Arguments that unwanted children are more frequently abused are without significant support. Although there is some evidence that in low-income single-mother families, unplanned children are more likely to be abused, they are not more often neglected, and the relationship is indirect

(Zuravin, 1987; Zuravin, 1991). The common variable is large family size or possibly unrealistic expectations or pregnancy losses. Other authors find no relationship (Kotelchuk, 1982). We found that child wantedness changed significantly during pregnancy, but at no point was the unwanted child abused or neglected more often than the wanted child (Ney et al., 1986).

Studies of children born to women who were refused abortions (Forssamn and Thuwe, 1966; Matejeck et al., 1978) prove very little because it's not possible to compare the unwanted, not-aborted child to a later sibling. The constitution of the not-aborted child and the environment into which it has been born are both unique. It appears that most of those children were born under poor and/or tumultuous circumstances. It should be remembered that in the current Western social climate, where people are paying hard cash to surrogate mothers or going on long waiting lists to aaopt, there are few if any reasons why a child needs to be raised by a struggling single parent, or why motherhood should be compulsory.

If the evidence and deductions are correct, then abortion directly or indirectly contributes to child abuse and neglect by:

1. interfering with the formation of a protective bond between the infant and both parents;
2. changing the parental response to the helpless infant's cry from nurture to aggression or neglect;
3. lessening the amount of touching the child and of breast-feeding;
4. diminishing the partner's support of the mother;
5. devaluing the child and thus those who care for children;
6. creating a complicated grief for the mother, thus making her less aware of and less able to respond to the child's needs;
7. promoting depression in the mother for which children will tend to blame themselves.

Maybe the hypothesis that there is a causal relationship between abortion and child abuse is not proved, but is has raised sufficient reasonable doubt to warrant a reconsideration of the oft-stated argument that freely available abortion will stop child abuse and neglect. After all, the onus of proof lies with those who promote or perform any medical procedure to show beyond reasonable doubt that it is both safe and effective. This has never been done with abortion. Rather, the best evidence is that abortion is not therapeutic, and it is not safe, i.e., that it kills unborn babies, damages women's health, disrupts families, and makes thousands of other children both more susceptible and more vulnerable to child abuse and neglect.

REFERENCES

D.B. Benfield (1978), 'Grief response of parents to neonatal death and parent participation in deciding care', *Pediatrics* 62: 171-7.

C.G. Bergstrand, M. Forslund and E. Stibner (1979), 'Child abuse in Malme', *Acta Scand Suppl* 275: 108-11.

J. Bowlby (1960), 'Grief and mourning in infancy and early childhood', *Psychoanal Study Child* 15: 9-52.

C.F. Bradley (1984), 'Abortion and subsequent pregnancy', *Can J Psych* 29(10): 494-8.

V. Calef (1972), 'Hostility of parents of children: some notes on fertility, child abuse, and abortion', *Int J Psychoanal Psychother* 1: 79-96.

J.O. Cavenar, A.A. Mallbie and J. L. Sullivan (1978), 'Aftermath of abortion: anniversary depression and abdominal pain', *Bull Menninger Clin* 41: 433-8.

A.D. Colman and L.L. Colman (1971), *Pregnancy: the psychological experience* (New York: Herder and Herder).

J. Culberg (1971), 'Mental reactions of women to perinatal death', in S. Karger (ed.), *Psychosomatic Medicine in Obstetrics and Gynecology*, Basel.

M. Dennis (1976), *Necessity and sorrow, life and death in an abortion hospital* (New York: Basic Books).

B. Egeland and L.A. Sroufe (1981), 'Attachment and early maltreatment', *Child Dev* 52(1): 44-52.

D.M. Fergusson, L.J. Horwood, F.T. Shannon and J.M. Lawton (1989), 'The Christchurch Child Development Study: a review of epidemiological findings', *Paeditr Perinat Epidemial* 3: (3) 302-25.

V.J. Fontana and D.J. Bersharov (1977), *The maltreated child* (Springfield: Charles C. Thomas).

J. Forrest (1987), 'Unintended pregnancy among American women', *Family Planning Perspectives* 19: 76-7.

H. Forssman and I. Thuwe (1966), 'One hundred and twenty children born after application for therapeutic abortion refused', *Acta Psychiatrica Scandinavica* 42: 71-88.

S. Freud (1917), *Mourning and melancholia*, J. Strachey (ed.), standard edition, vol. 14, p. 249 (London: Hogarth).

C. Greenland (1973), *Child abuse in Ontario*, Research Report III. Toronto: Ontario Ministry of Community and Social Services.

E.C. Herrenkohl and R.C. Herrenkohl (1979), 'A comparison of abused children and their nonabused siblings', *J Child Psychiatry* 18: 260-9.

C.H. Kempe and F.C. Helfer (1972), *Helping the battered child and his family* (Philadelphia and Toronto: R.B. Lippincott).

I. Kent, R.C. Greenwood and W. Loeken-Nicholls (1978), 'Emotional sequelae of elective abortion', *B.C. Med J* 20: 118-19.

M.H. Klaus and J.H. Kennell (1976), *Maternal infant bonding* (St Louis: C.V. Mosby Company).

D.D. Knudsen (1988), 'Child maltreatment over two decades, chance or continuity', *Violence Vict* 3(2): 129-44.

M. Kotelchuck (1982), 'Child abuse and neglect: prediction and misclassification', in R.H. Starr, Jr. (ed.), *Child abuse prediction: policy implications*, pp. 67-104 (Cambridge MA: Ballenger Publishing Company.)

R. Kumar and K. Robinson (1978), 'Previous induced abortion and ante-natal depression in

primiparae: a preliminary report of a survey of mental health in pregnancy', *Psychol Med* 8: 711-15.
E. Lewis (1979), 'Mourning by the family after a stillbirth or neonatal death', *Arch Dis Child* 54: 303-6.
F. Lieh-Mak, S.Y. Chungl and Y.W. Liu (1983), 'Characteristics of child-battering in Hong Kong: a controlled study', *Br J Psychiatry* 142: 89-94.
H.P. Martin (ed.) (1976), *The abused child* (Cambridge: Ballinger Publishing Company).
Z. Matejeck, Z. Dytrych and V. Schuller (1978), 'Children from unwanted pregnancies', *Acta Psychiatrica Scandinauica* 42: 71-88.
P.G. Ney (1979), 'Relationship between abortion and child abuse', *Can J Psychiatry* 24: 610-19.
_____ (1983), 'A consideration of abortion survivors', *Child Psychiatr Human Dev* 14: 158-79.
_____ (1987), 'Does verbal abuse leave deeper scars: a study of children and parents', *Can J Psychiatr* 32: 371-8.
_____ (1988a), 'Triangles of child abuse: a model of maltreatment', *J Child Abuse and Negl* 12: 363-73.
_____ (1988b), 'Transgenerational child abuse', *Child Psychiat Hum Dev* 18: 151-68.
_____ (1989), 'Child mistreatment: possible reasons for its transgenerational transmission', *Can J Psychiatr* 34: 594-601.
_____ (1992), 'Transgenerational triangles of abuse: a model of family violence', in Emilio C. Viano (ed.), *Intimate Violence: Interdisciplinary Perspectiues* (Washington: Hemisphere Publishing Corporation).
P.G. Ney, T. Fung and A.R. Wickett (1992), 'Causes of child abuse and neglect', *Can J Psychiatry* 37(6): 401-5.
P.G. Ney and J.A. Herron (1985), 'Children in crisis: to whom should they turn?', *NZ Med J* 98: 283-6.
P.G. Ney, J. McPhee, C. Moore and P. Trought (1986), 'Child abuse: a study of the child's perspective', *Child Abuse and Negl* 10: 511-18.
P.G. Ney, A. Peters (1995), 'Ending the Cycle of Abuse', Brunner/Mazel: New York.
P.G. Ney and A.R. Wickett (1989), 'Mental health and abortion: review and analysis', *Psych Journal U of Ottawa* 14: 506-16.
C.B. Pare and R. Hermione (1970), 'Follow-up of patients referred to terminatiun of pregnancy', *Lancet* 1: 635-7.
T. Tonkin (1979), 'Mortality in childhood', *B.C. Med Assoc J* 21: 212.
A. Troisi, F. Aureli, P. Piovesan and F.R. D'Amato (1989), 'Severity of early separation and later abusive mothering in monkeys: what is the pathogenic threshold?' *J Child Psychol Psychiatry* 30(2): 277-84.
S.J. Zuravin (1987), 'Unplanned pregnancies, family planning problems, and child maltreatment', *Family Relations* 36: 135-9.
_____ (1991), 'Unplanned childbearing and family size: their relationship to child neglect and abuse', *Fam Plann Perspect* 23(4): 155-61.

Methodological considerations in empirical research on abortion

RACHEL L. ANDERSON, DAVID C. HANLEY,
DAVID B. LARSON, ROGER C. SIDER

INTRODUCTION

Research emphasis on the effects of elective abortion has changed over the last two decades, due in part to the development of new medical reproductive techniques, the changing roles of women in society, and public debate concerning the morality of abortion as a viable choice of pregnancy termination. Early research on the contextual nature of the abortion experience was focused on the woman's decision regarding her pregnancy. (Speckhard, 1987). The outcome emphasis in this phase of research concentrated on adverse clinical effects, including psychiatric or medical complications of the abortion procedure (Adler, 1975; Cohen and Roth, 1984; Major, Mueller and Hildebrandt, 1985). More recently, research has begun to examine more fully the psychological sequelae and antecedents that affect a woman who seeks an abortion (Dagg, 1991).

In spite of the growing literature on the psychological responses to abortion, numerous methodological difficulties face researchers attempting to understand the abortion experience. Reviews of the literature have documented several methodological flaws which hinder research development. Lyons et al. (1988) suggest that while studies have surveyed women from a period of hours after the abortion to ten years after their most recent abortion, most studies covered a year or less following the abortion experience. For example, measuring immediate post-abortion responses, Cohen and Roth (1984) investigated intrusion, avoidance, depression, and anxiety five hours post-abortion. Results indicate a significant improvement on these measures in women undergoing abortion procedures. Moseley et al. (1981) also found lower scores on measures of depression and anxiety when examining women prior to discharge after the abortion procedure. While prospective studies over the immediate course of the abortion provide some evidence that women feel relieved by the surgical abortion procedure, they do not provide adequate knowledge about the mental health impact of the abortion after a much longer time has elapsed. As it is a surgical procedure it is expected that women undergoing abortion will have some anticipatory anxiety and distress regarding the safety of the procedure. These anticipatory emotions should remediate rapidly once the procedure has been completed. Thus, comparisons of emotional states immediately before and after the abortion should show relief and lowered distress. It would thus be some time later that psychological sequelae might likely manifest resulting from regret, guilt or other thoughts and feelings concerning the abortion experience.

The timing of measurements as well as the lack of substantial follow-up time periods are not the only conundrum for researchers. Doane and Quigley (1981) criticized the lack of adequate control groups, a prevalence of poorly defined and measured symptoms, and unspecified indications for the abortion. Studies examining mental health outcomes without comparison or control groups have tended to report a lack of significant negative responses in women. Cohen and Roth (1984) found lower scores on intrusion, avoidance, depression, and anxiety when measuring women five hours after the abortion procedure. Freeman et al. (1980) report that women undergoing their first abortion procedure had a significant reduction in scores on several scales including depression, anxiety, and an overall measure of emotional distress two weeks post-abortion. Major et al. (1985) assessed women immediately post-abortion and then again three weeks later. Results indicate that over this brief time period women's scores improved on depression, mood, and anticipated consequences. Finally, Jacobs et al. (1974) found significantly lower scores at one month post-abortion on measures of depression, symptoms, and mood. In contrast, Robbins (1979) did not find significant differences on outcomes between pre- and post-abortion periods. This study measured women at one year post-abortion specifically concerning their regret and willingness to repeat the abortion procedure. However, as this and the above studies all lacked appropriate comparison conditions, it is not possible to extrapolate what effects are due to the abortion and what are due to historical and maturational processes that were neither measured nor controlled (Cook & Campbell, 1979).

Identifying a reasonable comparison group for women who undergo an elective abortion is complicated by the fact that so many factors are involved in this decision. It is not possible ethically to randomly assign women seeking an abortion to one of two conditions: abortion versus no abortion; thus, an absolute control group study is difficult to obtain. Therefore, multiple approximations of such a control condition is needed. Some choices might be as follows:

Women who take their pregnancy to term
This group provides a comparison with women who do not seek an abortion. However, it is possible that they differ significantly from women seeking abortion on any number of psychological and socioeconomic variables. Also, those that choose parenting might have different outcomes than those who choose adoption.

Women who are denied abortion
This group appears an ideal comparison group *prima facie*; however, some notable differences may arise. It is likely that women who are denied abortions in circumstances where abortions are generally available might be different from women who chose to carry their pregnancy to term and as compared to women who received abortions. These differences must be better identified and understood. (Differences have been found between women who were denied abortion and women who experienced abortion procedures on outcome measures of mental disturbance and emotional strain: Hook, 1963; Drower & Nash, 1978a, 1978b; Pare & Raven, 1970; for more research examining outcomes of denied abortion, see Dagg 1991.)

In addition to problems with the timing of measurement and the use of comparison samples, many studies suffer from significant problems with the definitions of outcomes studied. A recent review by Anderson et al. (1994) reports little use in the published peer-reviewed research of careful diagnostic criteria to specify the prevalence of psychiatric conditions that might be associated with or attributable to the experience of undergoing a previous elective abortion. Specifically, the deficiency of studies utilising such diagnostic criteria does not allow for the estimation of the prevalence of depressive disorders or post-traumatic stress disorder. While a minority of studies use general measures of symptoms or mental health disorder screens, such as the Symptom Checklist 90 or the Beck Depression Inventory, these instruments are only general measures of distress and cannot be used to reliably detect diagnosable conditions. Since few would posit that every woman who undergoes an abortion is subject to a negative psychological outcome, measures that result in comparisons of means between groups may be inappropriate. Rather, research objectives need to be directed toward determining the level of risk for adverse psychological outcomes and what circumstances or predictors place women at increased risk for such adverse consequences.

Determining the prevalence of adverse psychological outcomes associated with abortion experiences and identifying risk factors predicting such outcomes requires careful sampling with measures assessing diagnostic outcomes, sufficient follow-up, and adequate comparison groups. Without appropriate comparisons it is not possible to understand any such estimates outside of the context of a single, non-generalisable sample. The present chapter strives to provide a methodological framework and an illustrative study with which to approach the study of the psychological consequences of abortion.

The published psychological effects of elective abortion are varied, ranging from positive, relieving effects to significant psychological distress and disorder. While this entire continuum merits examination, the focus of this chapter is on designing a research study to assess psychopathology and psychological distress. Ney et al. (1994) estimate that 25 per cent of women who have had pregnancy losses feel they need professional help. These authors report that women who abort electively appear to require more frequent and more sophisticated grief counseling than those who suffer other types of pregnancy loss (e.g., stillbirth, miscarriage). Further, data reported by the American Psychological Association (1987) suggest that distress prevalence rates in the United States range from 0.5 per cent to 15 per cent. While most women who undergo abortions do not have negative psychological reactions, these data suggest that some women do experience negative psychological sequelae secondary to the abortion experience. These data indicate that rates of abortion-related distress occur with sufficient frequency to merit scientific investigation. Further, a detailed examination of the methodological issues facing researchers investigating negative psychological reaction will likely aid in future prevention and treatment efforts.

Part of the difficulty confronting those who wish to study the effects of pregnancy decisions is a failure to elaborate the variables that influence the course and outcome of this process. To this end, Figure 1 displays a theoretical model which presents a sequence of factors in order to focus methodological considerations for research on the psychological effects of abortion. A woman's route from pregnancy decision to post-abortion involves a multi-stage process of choices and influences both implicit and explicit, active and passive. Such influences include previous psychiatric difficulties, social support, and issues contributing to the pregnancy decision.

INDIVIDUAL CHARACTERISTICS

Informing the understanding of how a woman decides on an abortion to terminate her pregnancy is a host of individual characteristics of that woman comprising her personality, history, and environment. Her beliefs and experiences inform her choice. The meaning of pregnancy and parenting also contribute. Speculating every potential contributing factor is of course impossible to elaborate and goes clearly beyond the focus of this chapter. However, since the present focus is on psychological outcomes, perhaps the most salient individual characteristic that must be considered is the woman's

Figure 1: Theoretical model of Pregnancy Decision-Making and Resolution

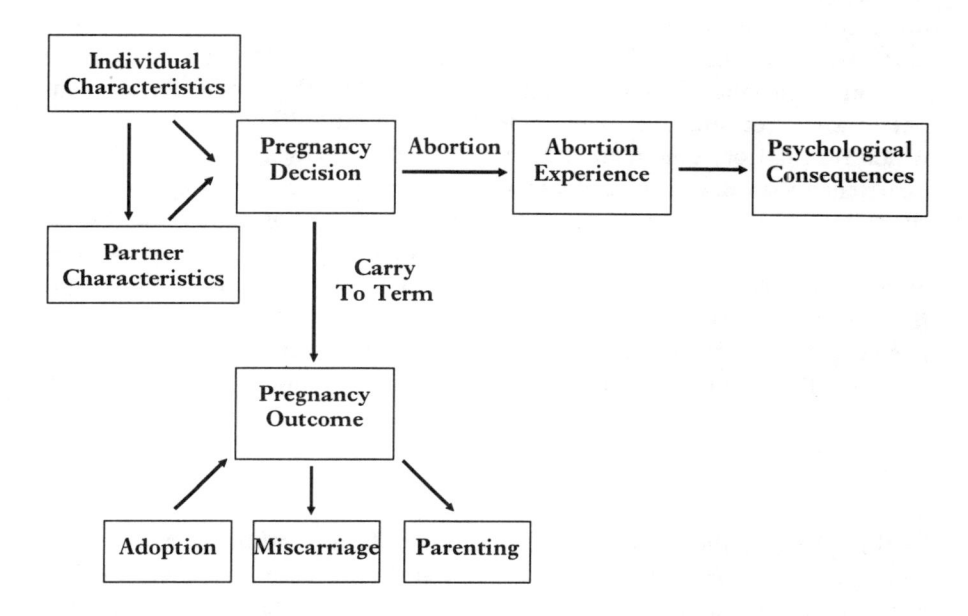

```
┌─────────────────┐
│   Individual    │
│ Characteristics │─┐
└─────────────────┘ │    ┌───────────┐  Abortion  ┌───────────┐    ┌───────────────┐
         │          └───▶│ Pregnancy │───────────▶│  Abortion │───▶│ Psychological │
         │          ┌───▶│  Decision │            │ Experience│    │  Consequences │
         ▼          │    └───────────┘            └───────────┘    └───────────────┘
┌─────────────────┐ │         │
│     Partner     │─┘         │  Carry
│ Characteristics │            │  To Term
└─────────────────┘            │
                               ▼
                        ┌───────────┐
                        │ Pregnancy │
                        │  Outcome  │
                        └───────────┘
                        ╱     │     ╲
                       ╱      │      ╲
              ┌─────────┐ ┌──────────┐ ┌──────────┐
              │ Adoption│ │Miscarriage│ │Parenting │
              └─────────┘ └──────────┘ └──────────┘
```

psychological wellbeing or adjustment prior to the pregnancy. The relatively low levels of both physical and psychological risk associated with elective abortion found in the published literature (Anderson et al., 1994) suggest that factors apart from the procedure *per se* may be responsible for post-abortion distress. It appears that certain factors, such as previous psychiatric difficulties, put women at greater risk for poor psychological adjustment (Dagg, 1991). If prior psychological difficulties precurse negative or clinically harmful reactions to abortion, then it would be reasonable to propose that psychological processes play an important role in mediating women's response. This suggests that the process of coping with the abortion experience may vary across women dependent on the prior psychiatric difficulties. Prior psychiatric difficulties including treatment or a disorder may predict or be a risk factor for post-abortion emotional sequelae. Alternatively, those with greater psychological resources would be better able to cope with the experience.

PARTNER CHARACTERISTICS

One of the least studied aspects of the psychological effects of abortion is on the contribution of the male partner to the woman's post-abortion adjustment. It goes without saying that all pregnancies result from the actions of both a woman and a man. However, these actions can vary quite dramatically based on the nature of the relationship between the two people involved. For women in an ongoing relationship, the male's support for and participation in the decision to abort and the surgical procedure itself may play an important role (Ney et al., 1994). On the other hand, for women not in a relationship, the male's role may be quite different. A pregnancy which results from one of any number of partners is likely a quite different experience than one that results from a monogamous relationship. In these situations the male's participation may be less relevant or impossible. For a pregnancy that results from rape, the male's participation could be considered wholly negative for the woman. Thus consideration of the nature of the woman's relationship to the impregnating male and that man's role in her pregnancy decision-making is a potentially important source of understanding the woman's eventual psychological adjustment to the elective abortion.

PREGNANCY DECISION LEADING TO ABORTION

In this phase of the sequence, many complex factors influence a women's decision to abort or carry the fetus to term, including access, finances, health knowledge, values and attitudes. For example, concerning a woman's abortion decision-making, research indicates that a longer waiting period between conception and abortion may result in higher levels of psychological stress on the woman. Research by Adler (1975) suggests that women who received first-trimester abortions experienced less difficulty with the decision to abort as compared to women who received mid-trimester abortions. This author also reported that women experiencing mid-trimester abortions were more likely to experience negative reactions post-abortion (see also Athanasiou et al., 1973).

Finally factors surrounding the access, expense, and availability of abortion and adoption services are likely to influence decision-making. Cultural and lifestyle considerations also inform these decisions (Hanley et al., 1994).

ABORTION EXPERIENCE

Conceptual and theoretical models of response to abortion are helpful in guiding and structuring research initiatives. Such models aid researchers to adequately define predictors and outcomes and measure symptoms and diagnoses with objective standards allowing for reliable, replicable measurement and study. (However, caution warrants discarding all facts relevant to a particular theory once that theory comes under review and is discarded. Some findings are dependable, others are not: Cook and Campbell, 1979.) Findings supported by replication of experimental results can be reinterpreted in an attempt to frame new theories. At least three psychological models appear relevant to the consideration of women's psychological reactions to abortion; 1) post-traumatic stress disorder, 2) stress and coping, and 3) existential/moral guilt.

The Post Traumatic Stress Disorder (PTSD) model assumes a diagnosable psychiatric disorder which results from a traumatic experience. In order to explain reactions to abortion within this model, DSM-IV criteria (Diagnostic Manual of the American Psychiatric Association, 4th edition) require that the experience of the abortion be traumatic for the women and that the symptoms following the abortion be consistent with the symptom profile of PTSD and include persistent re-experiencing of the abortion, persistent avoidance of stimuli associated with the abortion, and persistent symptoms of increased arousal (DSM-IV, 1994).

The stress and coping model suggests that abortion is an event experienced at differing levels of stress to each woman and that a woman's coping style and resiliency would predict her response to the abortion experience. Insufficient ability to cope with an abortion experience is influenced by a complex interaction of various life factors including insufficient social support and psychosocial instability (Adler and Dolcini, 1986; Major et al., 1994), coercion by significant others to abort (Watters, 1980), and concomitant stress due to other major life events (Blumberg and Golbus, 1975; Moseley et al., 1981). Using this model, a woman would be at risk for adverse psychological outcome if she experienced the abortion as stressful and had poor coping abilities and limited social skills or available social support.

Finally, the existential/moral model suggests that health psychological adjustment to abortion would result if the woman were minimally moral conflicted or sufficiently morally comfortable with her decision and did not experience her choice as personally unacceptable in terms of her beliefs about the abortion. However, if the decision to abort conflicted with her moral beliefs and/or values, then the woman would be at risk for poor emotional adjustment to the extent that she did not resolve her choice to abort in a manner consistent with her values and beliefs about abortion.

PINE REST STUDY

To address some of the methodological issues facing researchers examining mental health outcomes associated with abortion, we present the design of an American study of post-abortion stress conducted at Pine Rest Christian

Hospital, located in Grand Rapids, Michigan. This study was designed to examine potential risk factors for long-term abortion-related distress in women. Specifically, this study tested whether or not women who reported distress from their abortion experience fit a profile consistent with PTSD or an alternative model.

One treatment and two comparison groups were utilized. The two control groups helped to separate the effects attributable to the abortion from the effects attributable to irrelevancies that may have been associated with the abortion experience. Given the recognized risk for post-abortion in women with a history of psychiatric problems, three groups of women who were receiving outpatient psychiatric services were compared.

The treatment group was composed of a group of women who presented with a positive history of elective abortion and sought psychiatric services in response to negative psychological adjustment to abortion. The first control group also presented with a positive history of elective abortion; however, reasons for seeking outpatient services were not abortion related. The second control group sought outpatient services but denied any history of prior elective abortion. The average length of time across the experimental and first control groups between the abortion procedure and the research interviews was approximately nine years.

MEASURES

The selection of measures was guided by the principle of building on existing clinical and theoretical knowledge. Where possible, widely used measures with established reliability and validity were employed.

To assess PTSD symptomatology, the PTSD module of the Structured Clinical Interview for DSM-III-R (SCID-R; Spitzker, Williams and Gibbon, 1987), the MMPI-2 PK (Post-Traumatic Stress Disorder Scale) and PS (Post-Traumatic Stress Disorder Scale) scales (Keane, Malloy and Fairbank, 1984; Schlenger and Kulka, 1987), the Los Angeles Symptom Checklist (LASC; Leskin & Foy, 1993), and the Impact of Event Scale (IES; Horowitz, Wilner & Alvarez, 1979) were utilized.

Employing several measures of PTSD symptomatology, each having different methods of recording responses, addressed primary threat to the construct validity of any measurement procedure as discussed by Cook and Campbell (1979). These authors report the importance of mono-method bias in experimental research, stating that bias may occur when employing only one method of recording responses. The rationale is that the method is itself an irrelevancy (that no single method, e.g. self-report, is perfect) whose influence cannot be dissociated from the influence of the target construct, in this case the assessment of PTSD symptomatology. Cook and Campbell suggest implementing several methods of measuring a construct to alleviate the concern of mono-method bias. We address this concern in the design of the Pine Rest study by utilising four measures of PTSD symptomatology present in different forms; clinically structured interviews, semi-structured interview, and self-report measures.

Other measures used in the study that assessed stress and coping perspectives were the Interview for Recent Life Events (IRLE Paykel, 1974) which assessed the number and severity of stressful life events and the Social Support Questionnaire-6 (SSQ-6; Sarason, Sarason, Shearin & Pierce, 1987) which assessed the number of persons within one's social network perceived to be potential sources of social support, and one's satisfaction with the quality and extent of that social support.

Finally, the Abortion-Related Psychosocial History Interview (ARPHI; based in part on Speckhard's (1987) work) was designed for the study to gather intormation concerning the abortion experience including moral belief variables. While it is generally ill-advised to develop a measure specifically for a single study, the absence of relevant measures of abortion-relevant moral beliefs required the construction of this questionnaire.

RESULTS

The findings indicated a significantly higher rate of PTSD, as measured by the SCIDR, the LASC, and the Impact of Events Scale, among the abortion-distressed group as compared to women with a history of abortion who were seeking outpatient services for other problems. In fact, 73 per cent of women in the distressed group met the SCID-R criteria for PTSD. A significant difference was also found between the abortion-distressed women and the abortion-non-distressed women on a measure of moral belief. Women in the abortiondistressed group more often reported that they believed abortion to be morally wrong. There were no significant differences among groups on measures of psychopathology as measured by the MMPI-2, on overall social support, or religiosity. Further, abortion-distressed women experienced fewer recent adverse life events as compared to the abortion-nondistressed women.

Thus, the data suggest that some women experience PTSD as a result of elective abortion. It appears that this experience is not mediated by social support, other psychopathology, or life events. It does appear that the occurrence of PTSD might be related to a woman's experience of the abortion as outside her normal values or morality.

DISCUSSION

The Pine Rest study addressed several methodological considerations including the use of adequate control groups, reliable diagnostic criteria, and use of a theoretical model to direct research initiatives. This study also partially addressed the issue of adequate follow-up time periods. The finding that PTSD related to the abortion experience was present nearly a decade after the abortion demonstrates the importance of long-term follow-along studies. On the other hand, the study did not address when the PTSD developed over this time course. Future research should identify when at-risk women develop PTSD from abortion. Research that follows women for only a short time following the procedure may miss the development of PTSD altogether.

Additional limitations remain evident. The Pine Rest study was a retrospective analysis evaluating psychiatric symptoms years after the abortion experience. Although such a design provides an important contribution to the overall understanding of post-abortion distress, such an design precludes determining whether the development of PTSD is related to the individual's emotional, response at the time of the abortion. Prospective longitudinal designs that assess both the woman's experience of the abortion and her long-term adjustment, are needed to better understand factors that may place some women at greater risk for PTSD. Longitudinal studies, however, can be time consuming and expensive. Researchers need to consider the amount of time that will elapse between planning a longitudinal study and obtaining the results. It is likely that several years may pass between the conception of the experiment and the availability of results. When decisions have to be made quickly, such as policy decisions, researchers must weigh the advantages and disadvantages of different experimental designs that may best address timely concerns and be most suitable.

A second limitation is that the entire SCID was not given to participants; the SCID PTSD module was utilized alone. As Southwick et al. (1993) reports, high rates of comorbid psychopathology have been associated with PTSD including major depression and substance abuse. However, the presence of co-morbid psychopathology not assessed in this study does not rule out the existence of PTSD. Future research should examine the effects of co-occurring disorders to better understand potentially more severe levels of diagnostic distress experienced by some women who have undergone previous abortion procedures. A more extensive understanding of PTSD and possible co-occurring disorders would provide clinicians with a more comprehensive understanding of women with abortion experiences seeking mental health services. Such understanding would aid in the development of more effective assessment, prevention, and treatment efforts for these women.

Third, the sample in the Pine Rest study was gathered to specifically over-sample women who acknowledged that they had experienced difficulties in adjustment to their postabortion experience. It is important to note that while the findings indicate that PTSD can result from a prior elective abortion, there is no evidence from the data on how frequently such a reaction might be observed. In an attempt to address such a concern, a longitudinal study of randomly selected women seeking abortion services could be conducted. From such a design, one would be able to assess the frequency of observed PTSD development.

Significant methodological difficulties face researchers attempting to better understand psychological reactions associated with the abortion experience. In this chapter we have outlined a framework for better designs of research studies, thus improving research in this complicated arena. It appears clear that not every woman who undergoes an abortion has psychological difficulties. On the other hand, significant psychiatric problems can result from this experience. With careful selection of measures, assessment points, and comparison groups, an understanding of which women are at-risk for the development of adverse psychological sequelae of abortion can be achieved.

REFERENCES

N.E. Adler (1975), 'Emotional responses of women following therapeutic abortion', *American Journal of Orthopsychiatry*, 45, 446-54.

N.E. Adler and P. Dolcini (1986), 'Psychological issues in abortion for adolescents' in G.B. Melton (ed.), *Adolescent abortion; psychological and legal issues* (University of Nebraska Press, Lincoln, Nebraska).

American Psychiatric Association, *Diagnostic and Statistical Manual of Mental Disorders*, 4th ed. (American Psychiatric Association Press, Washington, DC).

American Psychological Association (1987), 'The psychological sequelae of abortion', Research review presented to the Office of the Surgeon General of the United States of America on behalf of the Public Interest Directorate of the American Psychological Association.

R.L. Anderson, J.S. Lyons and D.B. Larson (1994) 'A systematic review of the physical, psychological, and social impact of elective abortion on women. Paper presented to the American Psychological Association's conference on Psychosocial and Behavioral Factors in Women's Health: Creating an agenda for the 21st century' (Washington, DC, May).

R. Athanasiou, W.C. Oppel and L. Michelson, et al. (1973), 'Psychiatric sequelae to term birth and induced early and late abortion: a longitudinal study', *Family Planning Perspectives*, 5, 227-31.

B.D. Blumberg, M.S. Golbust and K.H. Hanson (1975), 'The psychological sequelae of

abortion performed for a genetic indication', *American Journal of Obstetrics and Gynecology*, 122, 799-808.
T. Cohen and S. Roth (1984), 'Coping with abortion', *Journal of Human Stress*, 10, 140-5.
T. Cook and D.T. Campbell (1979), *Quasi-experimentation. Design and analysis issues for field setting* (New York: Houghton, Miflin).
P.K.B. Dagg (1991), 'The psychological sequelae of therapeutic abortion—denied and completed', *American Journal of Psychiatry*, 148, 578-85.
B.K. Doane and B.G. Quigley (1981), 'Psychiatric aspects of therapeutic abortion', *Canadian Medical Association*, 125, 427-32.
S.J. Drower and E.S. Nash (1978a), 'Therapeutic abortion on psychiatric grounds, part I: A local study', *South African Journal of Medicine*, 54, 604-8.
S.J. Drower and E.S. Nash (1978b), 'Therapeutic abortion on psychiatric grounds, part II: The continuing debate'. *South African Journal of Medicine*, 54, 643-7.
E.W. Freeman and K. Rickels, G.R. Huggins, C.R. Garcia and J. Polin (1980), 'Emotional distress patterns among women having first or repeat abortions', *Obstetrics and Gynecology*, 55, 630-6.
D.C. Hanley, R.L. Anderson, D.B. Larson and R.C. Sider (1994), 'Post-traumatic Abortion Related Stress in Psychiatric Outpatients: Comparisons among Abortion-Distressed, Abortion-Non-Distressed, and No Abortion Group', submitted for publication.
K. Hook (1963), 'Refused abortion. A follow-up study of 249 women whose applications were refused by the National Board of Health in Sweden', *Acta Psychiatrica Scandinavia*, 168, 3-156 (Suppl).
M. Horowitz, H. Wilner and W. Alvarez (1979), 'Impact of Events Scale: A measure of subjective stress', *Psychosomatic Medicine*, 41, 209-18.
D. Jacobs, C.R. Garcia, K. Rickels and R.W. Preucel (1974), 'A prospective study on the psychological effects of therapeutic abortion', *Comprehensive Psychiatry*, 15, 423-34.
T.M. Keane, P.F. Malloy and J.A. Fairbank (1984), 'Empirical development of an MMPI subscale for the assessment of combat-related posttraumatic stress disorder', *Journal of Consulting and Clinical Psychology*, 52, 888-91.
G. Leskin and D. Foy (1993), 'The Los Angeles Symptom Checklist. Paper presented at the 9th annual meeting of the International Society for Traumatic Stress Studies' (San Antonio, TX).
J.S. Lyons, D.B. Larson, W.M. Huckeba, J.L. Rogers and C.P. Mueller (1988), 'Research on the psychosocial impact of abortion: A systematic review of the literature 1966 to 1985', in G.P. Reiger (ed.), *Values and Public Policy, Family Research Council* (Washington, DC).
B. Major, J.M. Zubek, L. Cooper and C. Cozzarelli (1994), 'Social conflict, social support, and adjustment to abortion. Paper presented to the American Psychological Association's conference on Psychosocial and Behavioral Factors in Women's Health: Creating an agenda for the 21st century' (Washington DC, May).
B. Major, P. Mueller and K. Hildebrandt (1985), 'Attributions, expectations, and coping with abortion', *Journal of Personality and Social Psychology*, 48, 585-99.
O.T. Moseley, D.R. Follingstad, H. Harley and R. Heckel (1981), 'Psychological factors that predict reaction to abortion', *Journal of Clinical Psychology*, 37, 276-9.
P.G. Ney, T. Fung, A.R. Wickett and C. Beamon-Dodd (1994), 'The effects of pregnancy loss on women's health', *Social Science Medicine*, 38, 1193-1200.
C.M.B. Pare and H. Raven (1970), 'Psychiatric sequelae to therapeutic abortion: Follow-up of patients referred for termination of pregnancy', *Lancet*, 1, 635-8.

E.S. Paykel (1974), 'Life stress and psychiatric disorder: Application of the clinical approach' in B.P. Dohrenwend and B.S. Dohrenwend (eds.), *Stressful life events: Their nature and effects*, pp. 135-49 (New York: Wiley).

J.M. Robbins (1979), 'Objective versus subjective responses to abortion', *Journal of Consulting and Clinical Psychology*, 47, 994-5.

I.G. Sarason, B.R. Sarason, E.N. Shearin and G.R. Pierce (1987), 'A brief measure of social support: Practical and theoretical limitations', *Journal of Social and Personal Relationships*, 4, 497-510.

W.E. Schlenger and R.A. Kulka (1987), 'Performance of the Keane-Fairbank MMPI Scale and other self-report measures in identifying post-traumatic stress disorder'. Paper presented at the American Psychological Association annual meeting (New York).

S.M. Southwick, R. Yehuda and E.L. Giller (1993), 'Personality disorders in treatment-seeking combat veterans with posttraumatic stress disorder', *American Journal of Psychiatry*, 150, 1020-3.

A. Speckhard (1987), *Psychosocial stress following abortion* (Sheed & Ward, Kansas City, Missouri).

R.L. Spitzer, J.B.W. Williams and M. Gibbon (1987), *Structured Clinical Interview for DSM-III-R* (patient version). New York: New York State Psychiatric Institute.

W.W. Waters (1980), 'Mental health consequences of abortion and refused abortion', *Canadian Journal of Psychiatry*, 25, 68-73.

List of contributors

RACHEL L. ANDERSON is presently a doctoral student in the Human Development and Social Policy Program at Northwestern University, Evanston, Illinois. Her research focus is on women's health, including completion of a systematic review of the medical, psychological and social effects of induced abortion on women, funded by the US Department of Health and Human Services.

CHARLES BLACKER, MB, BS, FRCPsych., completed his medical training at Guy's Hospital and subsequent psychiatric training at both Guy's Hospital and St Bartholomew's under Professor Anthony Clare. Following an MD thesis in General Practice and Epidemiology he is now a General Psychiatrist and Liaison Psychiatrist at the Royal Cornwall Hospital, Truro. He was instrumental in the design and setting up of a prospective study of the Psychological Sequelae of Abortion conducted by Dr Gabriella Zolese, Springfield Hospital, Tooting. He is a Senior Lecturer at the University of Bristol and is actively involved as advisor to various bodies including the House of Lords Select Committee on Abortion, the Church of England, and the Evangelical Alliance.

PATRICIA CASEY, MD, FRCPsych., qualified at University College, Cork, in 1976. She trained in psychiatry in Nottingham and Edinburgh. She has researched into suicide, personality disorders and a range of other psychiatric issues. Author of *A Guide to Psychiatry in Primary Care* and *Social Functioning: the hidden axis of psychiatric classification*. She was appointed Professor of Psychiatry, University College Dublin in 1992 Her wide clinical experience includes, in particular, the treatment of the psychological aftermath of induced abortion.

PETER DOHERTY, MRCS, LRCP, DTM&H, worked for many years as a health advisor and in hospital in the Middle East and Africa before taking up medical practice in London. The author of several pamphlets on bio-ethical subjects, he is currently the editor of the *Catholic Medical Quarterly* and a governor of the Linacre Centre for Health Care Ethics.

TAK FUNG, BSc, MSc, PhD, received his pure mathematics degrees from the National Taiwan University (BSc) and the University of Windsor (MSc). He received his statistics degree from the University of Calgary (PhD). His research interest is the bio-statistical area. Dr Fung has published scientific articles in journals including the *Journal of Neurology, British Journal of Obstetrics and Gynaecology, International Journal of Child Abuse and Neglect, Canadian Journal of Psychiatry, Pre- and Perinatal Psychology Journal*, and *Social Science and Medicine*. He worked as a bio-statistician at Dalhousie University during the early to mid 1980s and is currently a senior statistical consultant/bio-statistician, University Computing Services, University of Calgary.

SANDRO GINDRO, MA, PhD, studied under Professor Nicola Abbagnano in Turin. His psychoanalytical training was completed with the Fruedian Italian Society of Psychoanalysis. In 1976 Professor Gindro established the Psychoanalytic Institute for Social Research (IPRS). He is President of Committee on Xenophobia and Racism established by the Italian Ministry of Social Affairs. Since 1993 he has been in charge of teaching Psychoanalysis of Pregnancy at the Post Graduate School of Gynaecology and Obstetrics of the University 'La Sapienza' of Rome.

MARY A. GREENWOLD is the reseach coordinator for the National Institute for Healthcare Research. The impact of religious commitment on physical and mental health as well as social status is one of her top research interests. She specialises in the use of the systematic review methodology in areas of public policy controversy such as religion, abortion, school-based clinics and criminal behaviour.

DAVID C. HANLEY, MSW, is a Senior Clinical Social Worker at Pine Rest Christian Hospital in Grand Rapids, Michigan. Trained at the University of Michigan Graduate School of Social Work, he has specialised in the treatment of women stressed by their abortions and has served as principal investigator of a clinical research study of post-abortion stress conducted at Pine Rest Christian Hospital.

DAVID B. LARSON, MD, MSPH, is Adjunct Professor of Psychiatry at Duke University Medical Center, Northwestern University Medical School, and the United States Uniformed Health Service. A former research psychiatrist at the National Institutes of Mental Health, the National Institutes of Health, and the US Department of Health and Human Services, he is now President of the National Institute for Healthcare Research. Dr Larson helped to develop the systematic review methodology and specialises in the public policy implication of religious commitment. He has over 160 professional publications in such policy areas as mental health diagnoses and services, use of nursing homes, and AIDS/HIV infection.

JOHN S. LYONS is Associate Professor of Psychiatry and Medicine at Northwestern University Medical School. He is currently the Faculty Director of the Thresholds National Research and Training Center, a US Department of Education (NIDRR) center for the study of psychosocial rehabilitation for persons with serious mental illness. He has more than 100 professional publications in the areas of mental health services and the relationship of religion to health and well-being.

List of contributors

PHILIP G. NEY, MA, MD, FRCP(C), FRANZCP, graduated in medicine from the University of British Columbia and trained as a child psychiatrist and child psychologist at McGill University, the University of London and the University of Illinois. He has done research into child abuse for fifteen years and written over sixteen papers and a book on this subject. He has been a professor in five universities in four countries. His early research made him aware of the connection between child abuse and abortion. More recently he has studied children who are the survivors of abortion and has been conducting therapeutic groups for men and women abused as children. From that experience, a book *Ending the Cycle of Abuse: the stories of women abused as children and the group therapy techniques that helped them heal*, has recent been published by Brunner/Maxel, New York. Dr Ney is currently Clinical Professor, Faculty of Medicine, University of British Columbia.

VINCENT M. RUE, PhD, together with his wife Susan, are the directors of the Institute for Pregnancy Loss, Portsmouth, New Hampshire. The Insitute specialises in the evaluation of and the recovery from high-stress pregnancy loss, particularly traumatic abortion and adoption experiences. He has presented testimony on the psychological effect of abortion to committees in both the US Senate and House of Representatives. Dr Rue was also a consultant of the Office of the Surgeon General, US Public Health Service, on the Report ot the President on Abortion Morbidity. He was one of the first to identify clinically post-abortion trauma and develop diagnostic criteria for Post-abortion Syndrome.

KIMBERLY A. SHERRILL is a psychiatrist in private practice in Winston-Salem, North Carolina. A former Assistant Professor of Psychiatry and Behavioral Medicine at Bowman Gray School of Medicine, Dr Sherrill is a geriatrician and recently was awarded a Geriatric Mental Health Academic Award from NIMH for development of a programme of research focussed on the relationship between religion and aging, on of her top research interests.

ROGER C. SIDER, MD, is Medical Director of Pine Rest Christian Hospital in Grand Rapids, Michigan, and Professor of Psychiatry in the College of Human Medicine of Michigan State University. Trained at the University of Toronto and Johns Hopkins Hospital, he has published numerous articles and book chapters on psychiatric ethics and has a life-long interest in clinical care, clinical administration, and the interface of psychiatry and religion.

AGNETA SUTTON, Fil. Kand, MSc(Econ), MPhil, a bioethicist with a philosophical training, is a Research Fellow at the Centre for Bioethics and Public Policy, London (established in 1991 to promote research and debate from a Christian and Hippocratic position). She is the author of *Prenatal Diagnosis: Confronting the Ethical Issues* (London, 1990) and *Infertility and Assisted Conception: What you should know* (1993).

MARGARET WHITE, MB, ChB, DObst, RCOG, is a retired general practitioner and Vice-President of the Society for the Promotion of Unborn Children. She is a founder member of the World Federation of Doctors Who Respect Human Life. She was a magistrate for 28 years and deputy chairman of the Juvenile Bench. She was an elected member of the General Medical Council, 1984-89. She is the founder of the Anna Fund and author of *Two Million Silent Killings* and *Aid and the Positive Alternative*.

ADELE ROSE WICKETT, BSN, received her nursing degree from the University of British Columbia. She taught nursing in India before raising four daughters with her husband, Gary. Together they managed a bookstore in Victoria, BC, for many years. Adele has been involved in school board administration. Her other publications include several short stories, poetry, bio-history and travel articles in addition to research papers on child abuse.